CCBD

Council for
Children with
Behavioral
Disorders

UNDERSTANDING INDIVIDUAL DIFFERENCES

Highlights from the National Symposium on What Educators Should Know About Adolescents Who Are Gay, Lesbian, or Bisexual

Teachers College, Columbia University, New York City
February 1996

Sponsored by
Council for Children with Behavioral Disorders

EDITED BY

LYNDAL M. BULLOCK
UNIVERSITY OF NORTH TEXAS, DENTON

ROBERT A. GABLE
OLD DOMINION UNIVERSITY, NORFOLK, VIRGINIA

JOSEPH R. RIDKY
MONTGOMERY COUNTY PUBLIC SCHOOLS, MARYLAND

ABOUT THE COUNCIL FOR CHILDREN WITH BEHAVIORAL DISORDERS (CCBD)

CCBD is an international professional organization committed to promoting and facilitating the education and general welfare of children/youth with behavioral and emotional disorders. CCBD, whose members include educators, parents, mental health personnel, and a variety of other professionals, actively pursues quality educational services and program alternatives for persons with behavioral disorders, advocates for the needs of such children and youth, emphasizes research and professional growth as vehicles for better understanding behavioral disorders, and provides professional support for persons who are involved with and serve children and youth with behavioral disorders.

In advocating for the professionals in the field of behavioral disorders, CCBD (a division of The Council for Exceptional Children) endorses the Standards for Professional Practice and Code of Ethics which was adopted by the Delegate Assembly of The Council for Exceptional Children in 1983.

Other CCBD Products

- **Behavioral Disorders**

  This journal, published quarterly, serves as a means to exchange information and share ideas related to research, empirically tested educational innovations, and issues and concerns relevant to students with behavioral disorders. The journal is free with CCBD membership or is available to nonmembers by subscription.

- **Beyond Behavior**

  This practitioner-oriented journal is published three times annually and focuses on issues faced by direct service providers in the field. The journal is free with CCBD membership or is available to nonmembers by subscription.

- **CCBD Newsletter**

  The newsletter is designed to keep members informed about the organization and its activities and is available to members on a quarterly basis.

- **CCBD Monograph Series:**
  - Severe Behavior Disorders of Children and Youth
  - Programming for Adolescents with Behavioral Disorders
  - Monograph on Inclusion: Ensuring Appropriate Services to Children and Youth with Emotional/Behavioral Disorders - I*

  - Monograph on Inclusion: Ensuring Appropriate Services to Children and Youth with Emotional/Behavioral Disorders - II*
  - Perspectives on School Aggression and Violence: Highlights from the Working Forum on Children and Youth Who Have Aggressive and Violent Behaviors

- **Retrospective Series on Critical Issues in Emotional/Behavioral Disorders:**
  - Improving the Social Skills of Children and Youth with Emotional/Behavioral Disorders

- **Audiotapes on Inclusion:**
  - Ensuring Appropriate Services to Children and Youth with Emotional/Behavioral Disorders - I*
  - Ensuring Appropriate Services to Children and Youth with Emotional/Behavioral Disorders - II*

* The audiotapes feature the keynote speakers and the monographs highlight the speakers and the discussion groups for the two CCBD Working Forums on Inclusion held in St. Louis, MO, October 1, 1993 (Vol. I) and in Hartford, CT, March 25, 1994 (Vol. II).

All products are available from The Council for Exceptional Children, 1920 Association Drive, Reston, VA 20191, 703-620-3660.

CONTENTS

Preface / **v**

It's Like Opening Pandora's Box: Addressing the Needs of
Gay and Lesbian Adolescents Within Educational Systems / **1**
    Gerald P. Mallon

Making a Difference: A Call for Education and Action / **7**
    Eileen Bardwell Raymond

Youth and Homosexuality / **12**
    Ann Thompson Cook and Wayne Pawlowski

Gay, Lesbian, and Bisexual Adolescents: Finding Them,
Understanding Them, and Recognizing Their Potential / **21**
    Joseph R. Ridky

New Directions for Lesbian, Gay, and Bisexual Youth:
Reflections on the Harvey Milk School / **24**
    Joyce Hunter

Considerations in Working with Adolescents
Who Are Gay, Lesbian, or Bisexual / **28**
    Robert Rahamin, Philippe J. Dupont, and Tania DuBeau

Safe Supportive Schools for All Youth: A Call to Action / **32**
    Ann Fitzsimons-Lovett and Mary Gale Budzisz

Adolescents Who Are Gay, Lesbian, or Bisexual:
The Schools' Challenge / **36**
    Nomsa Gwalla-Ogisi and Shelly Sikorski

Creating Educational Environments That Value Gay and Lesbian Youth:
A Synopsis of a Panel Presentation / **41**
    Tom McIntyre and Joel Von Ornsteiner

Resources for Educators / **45**

PREFACE

In recent years, there has been extensive discussion about making schools more inclusive for all students. Earlier, the focus was on appropriate inclusion of students from ethnic and multicultural backgrounds. In the 1990s, focus shifted to creating more inclusive environments for students with disabilities. Few educators would take issue that *ALL* students are entitled to the most appropriate, safe, and supportive educational environment possible. No doubt, all would agree that the goal is to assist all children and youth to reach their maximum potential academically, emotionally, and socially.

Many of the changes that have occurred in education have been the result of effective community-based advocacy by groups of parents and others who have utilized their personal and political clout to ensure that the issues with which they are concerned are heard and acted upon. Unfortunately, there is at least one group of youth for whom widespread advocacy has, in general, been neglected in the communities and schools. That group may be referred to as sexual minority adolescents, including those who are gay, lesbian, bisexual, or those who are struggling with their sexual orientations.

The Council for Children with Behavioral Disorders (CCBD) has expressed concern about this group of young people, but not because students who are gay, lesbian, bisexual or who are struggling with their sexual identities are emotionally/behaviorally disordered. Rather because these students often are forced from their homes by nonaccepting parents; become runaways; become abusers of drugs or alcohol; attempt or complete suicide; become law breakers; or develop acting-out or withdrawn behaviors that result in aggressive or violent acts or low self-esteem. The majority of sexual minority youth simply remain "invisible," internalizing homophobic remarks and dealing quietly with self-esteem issues. It is important that educators understand the "uniqueness" of all individuals and have at hand ways to structure nurturing, supportive, and inclusive learning environments that are safe and nondiscriminatory. The challenge is to provide educators with information that will enable them to create school environments and adjust school curricula to acknowledge the existence and acceptability of students whose sexual orientations differ from the majority.

Many professionals have expressed concern about how to work effectively with adolescents who are gay, lesbian, or bisexual. CCBD responded to this concern by sponsoring a national symposium on "Understanding Individual Differences: What Educators Should Know About Adolescents Who Are Gay, Lesbian, or Bisexual," held in February 1996 at Teachers College, Columbia University, New York City. The symposium was designed to impart information to aid in a greater understanding of these youth from a social, psychological, and educational perspective with an emphasis on safety and nondiscrimination issues.

The highlights of the Symposium are reflected in this monograph. The papers presented here have been developed by the keynote speakers and facilitators of discussion groups. A resource section is included for readers who desire to enhance their knowledge on the subject. We believe the information provided to be informative and pertinent to the work of educators and other caregivers involved with adolescents who are gay, lesbian, or bisexual.

Lyndal M. Bullock
Robert A. Gable
Joseph R. Ridky
Editors

IT'S LIKE OPENING PANDORA'S BOX:
ADDRESSING THE NEEDS OF
GAY AND LESBIAN ADOLESCENTS
WITHIN EDUCATIONAL SYSTEMS

GERALD P. MALLON
COLUMBIA UNIVERSITY, NEW YORK CITY

It was horrible to be a gay kid in high school. I was always hiding, scared to death that someone would find out my secret. Most of the kids were pretty horrible to anyone who seemed gay. But I'll tell you who were the worst, the male gym teachers. They were always making fun of me and even called me a faggot. It was terrible [May, 1995].[1]

Unfortunately, many of our schools are not nurturing environments for gay and lesbian young people. Untrained and without policies to guide them, most teachers and other school personnel have no idea how to work with a self-identified young person who is gay or lesbian. Others, unable to identify these young people, because they look only for gender-nonconforming ways of dressing or mannerisms, are not convinced that they have any young people who are gay or lesbian within their systems.

The reality is that young people who are gay and lesbian have always been present in schools, but their existence usually has not been noted because they have been socialized to hide (Mallon, 1994; Martin, 1982). Marginalized by a society which, despite some social gains, continues to view homosexuality through a pejorative and stigmatizing lens, most young people who are gay and lesbian hide because they have determined that it is not safe to be open about their orientation. Although the literature concerning gay and lesbian adolescents within educational settings is limited (Harbeck, 1993; Jennings, 1994b), the literature with respect to gay and lesbian youth in general has grown exponentially (Gonsiorek, 1988; Hunter & Schaecher, 1987, 1990; Mallon, 1992, 1994; Remafedi, 1985, 1987a, 1987b; Savin-Williams, 1989, 1994, 1995; Schneider, 1988; Whitlock, 1989).

In this paper, I draw upon the literature from both domains and qualitative data analysis from interviews conducted with adolescents who are gay and lesbian and their families (Mallon, 1994) to examine the need to create gay- and lesbian-affirming environments within educational systems. Adopting an ecological perspective, I view the adolescent who is gay or lesbian through a wide lens that identifies the difficulties these young people experience as manifestations of the poor fit or lack of mutuality between them and their environments. Such a perspective creates a framework in which individuals and environments are understood as a unit, in the context of their relationship to one another (Germain, 1991). As such, within the context of educational systems, I will examine the primary reciprocal exchanges and transactions that gay or lesbian young people and their families face as they confront the unique person — environmental tasks involved in a society that assumes all of its members are heterosexual. Several areas that relate to this process are specifically explored, namely, the effects of developing a false self because of the socialization process of hiding, and the means by which adolescents adapt to their iden-

---

[1] All quotations are taken from interviews the author conducted with professionals who work with gay and lesbian adolescents and young people themselves. The bracketed information specifies the date of interviews in which the quoted comment was made. All names have been changed to protect the confidentiality of the clients.

tity, and finally, a review of recommendations for systemic changes that could create more nurturing environments for all people who interface with the educational system, including gay and lesbian adolescents and their families. Recommendations for competent educational practices with gay and lesbian adolescents and their families are also presented.

Official Invisibility and Homo-Ignorance

Today, the field of education faces many challenges in providing quality services to children and their families. Some educators have argued that in particular, the needs of students who are gay and lesbian have not been adequately served (Jennings, 1994b; Krysiak, 1987; Rofes, 1989). Unfortunately, there are few studies (Norris, 1992; Sears, 1992) which document the educational experiences for these young people. Educators generally have been reticent to address the issues of gay and lesbian adolescents and their families for two leading reasons: First, discussions about homosexuality continue to evoke a high level of discomfort, and as such, administration and school boards sanction a policy of "official invisibility." Secondly, because many educators within the field are customarily biased against and possess scant information about gay and lesbian individuals, these educators practice from a perspective of homo-ignorance. One educator I interviewed for a recent study illuminates this point further:

> No one talks about it, but gay and lesbian students are present in all schools. But it's never going to show up in the statistics. They don't have it documented that a girl is a lesbian in a high school, but she's there. Of course it's not documented, the message that gay and lesbian kids get is—hide it! It's like, as long as we don't have to know, it's all right. There's a certain tolerance if you don't really have to face what's happening, but somehow if you have to deal with the existence of gay and lesbian people, then all hell breaks loose. They just don't even want to hear those words—gay or lesbian. It's almost like they are saying—please don't make me go through that—don't come near me with that! But the thing is, they have gay kids in their schools and they don't even know it because all they know are the stereotypes of what they think gay and lesbian people are. They're afraid if they discuss it—they're afraid that if they talk about it openly, that it will be like opening Pandora's Box [March, 1993].

In Search of a "Good Fit"

As young people who are lesbian, gay, or bisexual strive for the best person-environment "fit," many find that as a consequence of their environment's intolerance, the fit is not good. Utilizing an ecological perspective suggested by Germain (1979), I propose an approach that suggests these young people have three strategies of adaptation from which to choose. A young person who is gay or lesbian may actively decide to adapt by attempting to change himself or herself. For example, the adolescent who is gay or lesbian might try to date opposite gendered individuals in an effort to change. Or, the individual may attempt to modify the environment. A person might look for cues within the various environments which signal that it is safe to disclose, or at least to explore, these options. Finally, some young people who are gay or lesbian may migrate to a new environment that could provide safety and sustain them with the nutrients necessary for health. That is, young people might leave home to seek other habitats or look for opportunities outside their school environments to find cultural niches with others who are like themselves.

Youth who are gay and lesbian must negotiate the dual stresses of living within a family system and attending school within an environment which generally is hostile to their very existence. As a consequence of living with this constant stress, many lesbian and gay youths search for ways to cope with their (sexual) identities. Tacitly understanding that the policy of official silence within both the family and the education systems causes them to constantly negotiate life within hostile environments, most young people who are gay or lesbian adapt by hiding. Hiding one's orientation, the adaptation choice, which almost all young gay and lesbian people initially select, leads to the development of a false sense of self (Shernoff & Finnegan, 1991). Others learn to sublimate their identity, either positively with academics, sports, school, or church clubs, or negatively by abusing alcohol and other substances, or by engaging in promiscuous sex with both genders. Still, a third group accepts their identity and, while attempting to live openly, may encounter both verbal harassment and physical violence. Whichever option they choose, lesbian and gay adolescents often fear losing their families and friendships if those who are important to them learn the truth about them.

Although some young people who are gay or lesbian can hide, others may not be able to do so if they have gender-nonconforming behaviors or ways of dressing. These young people, who may or may not be gay or lesbian—as gender-nonconforming behavior or styles of dress does not necessarily indicate one's sexual orientation—are perceived, nevertheless, by peers to be gay or lesbian and experience even greater stress because they cannot hide.

Such stigmatizing experiences, which are analogous to racism, sexism, ageism, classism and anti-Semitism, cause a great deal of stress for the gay or lesbian adolescent, who feels isolated, scared, and different. In many cases, this stigma leads to coping complications (Germain & Gitterman, 1980). Savin-Williams and Rodriguez (1993) assert that lesbian and gay youth of color face additional stress in developing a mature identity because they must integrate their ethnic, cultural, and racial background with their sexual orientation and identity. In all, for young people who are gay or lesbian, the stress of negotiating a life within a hostile environment is directly related to the lack of sustenance they have experienced within their families and in their schools.

A Systemic Model for Creating Affirming Environments

The report of the Massachusetts Governor's Commission on Gay and Lesbian Youth, "Making Schools Safe for Gay and Lesbian Youth" (Commonwealth of Massachusetts Governor's Commission on Gay and Lesbian Youth, 1993), provides several important guidelines for educators interested in addressing the needs of gay and lesbian youth and their families. The commission—a coalition of gay and lesbian students, parents of gay and lesbian students, educators, and human service professionals in Massachusetts—was a major step to breaking the silence surrounding gay and lesbian youth and their families. The first of its kind in the United States, the Massachusetts Commission can serve as a model for creating gay- and lesbian-affirming environments that other educators can emulate. The Massachusetts Commission report "outlines the problems faced by gay and lesbian youth in schools and makes a series of recommendations that guarantee safety and end abuse" (p. 159). What follows is a review of five recommendations from the commission, which can be used as a basis for creating gay- and lesbian-affirming environments in school systems.

Recommendation One: School Policies That Protect Students Who Are Gay and Lesbian

Professionals operating in the absence of clearly stated policies utilize their own personal experiences as a guide, which in the case of dealing with homosexually oriented youth can lead to conclusions based on cultural, religious, and societal biases. Written, formal policies help prevent discrimination, harassment, and verbal abuse of young people who are gay and lesbian and those perceived to be gay or lesbian. As such, schools should establish policies that ensure equal access to all courses and activities for all students. Adopting and publicizing policies which ban antigay language and harassment on the part of the faculty and students is a simple straightforward solution—one which sends a clear message to the school community and costs nothing to implement. Obvi-

ously, violence of any type should not be tolerated, and clear procedures should be established to deal with such incidents.

Recommendation Two: Suicide Prevention and Violence Prevention Training for Teachers and Counselors

An essential component in creating safer environments for students who are gay and lesbian is to ensure that all school personnel (e.g., teachers, administrators, cafeteria workers, maintenance and support staff) are equipped with accurate and relevant knowledge necessary to address the needs of gay and lesbian youth in a caring and sensitive manner. In addition to providing violence prevention and crisis intervention training for school personnel, educational systems must also become expert in marshaling community resources to meet the needs of gay and lesbian students and their families. Moreover, continued and ongoing education and training for all levels of education professionals is essential to raise the consciousness about the need to develop appropriate and safe environments for youth who are gay and lesbian.

If educators are truly committed to diversity, then they must be willing to address the issues of sexual diversity as well. The myths of child molestation (see de Young, 1982; Groth, 1978; Groth & Birnbaum, 1978; Newton, 1978) and "recruitment" of young people must also be directly confronted in order to overcome obstacles to providing competent services to young gays and lesbians and their families. Clinical theories which view homosexuality in developmentally pejorative terms and moralistic arguments must also emerge, so that they can be diffused and answered (Saperstein, 1981).

Recommendation Three: School-Based Support Groups for Students Who Are Gay and Straight

Young people respond best to other young people. One option is the development of weekly support groups for gay and lesbian adolescents and other students who want to talk about gay, lesbian, and related issues. Heterosexual young people also need opportunities to talk openly with their peers who are gay, lesbian, or bisexual. Gay/Straight alliances are effective in-school support groups. Schools need to commit resources to this effort by advertising the existence of the group and by appointing a faculty advisor to facilitate this process with the students. Because guidance counselors, nurses, and school social workers are frequently among the first to address issues of sexual orientation in school systems, these professionals should receive special training to provide support and information for gay and lesbian youth and their families (see Powell, 1987; Reynolds & Koski, 1993; Tartiagni, 1978).

Recommendation Four: Information in School Libraries for Adolescents Who Are Gay and Lesbian

Young people who are (or think they might be) gay or lesbian frequently do not have access to accurate information about their own social identity. Young people need to have access to information about gay and lesbian issues. Many resources are readily available in school libraries. Such information should include videos and books—especially those written by young people for young people (see Due, 1995)—as well as pamphlets and other materials for use by students, teachers, and parents. Indeed, information that is specifically written for the parents of lesbian and gay youth is especially important (see Borhek, 1983, 1988; Dew, 1994; Fairchild & Hayward, 1989; Griffin, Wirth, & Wirth, 1986; Parents and Friends of Lesbians and Gays, 1990; Strommen, 1989). Libraries should develop a reading list of books on gay and lesbian issues and should periodically display these books and materials in a highly visible way. Finally, a well-researched local guide to gay and lesbian youth organizations and organizations which support their family members should also be available.

Recommendation Five: Curriculum That Includes Content About People Who Are Gay and Lesbian

Because the classroom is the heart of the learning experience for students in educational systems, discussion about gay and lesbian issues and a recognition of the contribution of gay and lesbian people to history, literature, arts, science, and modern society should be integrated into all subject areas and departments in an age-appropriate fashion (see Jennings, 1994a). To accomplish this goal, educational systems must commit resources to examine current curriculum for bias, provide faculty development to assist teachers in developing competence in this area, and encourage and support teachers to attend conferences that focus on gay and lesbian issues relevant to their subject areas.

Recommendations for Competent Educational Practice with Gay and Lesbian Adolescents and Their Families

The following are recommendations for promoting competence with respect to working with gay and lesbian students and their families:

- Acknowledge that gay men and lesbians are your clients. The first step in providing competency-based services is to realize and acknowledge that not all students or parents are heterosexually oriented. In making an assessment of your students and parents, do not assume that all students or all parents are heterosexual. The only way that you will know someone's sexual orientation is if they tell you. Many times, professionals make assumptions based on inaccurate information or outmoded cues. Students and parents will tell you who they are when and if they feel ready. Students and parents will come out when they feel that a safe environment has been created for them in which to disclose. Whether you know it or not, you already have students and parents who are gay or lesbian.

- Continue to educate yourself and your coworkers about gay men and lesbians. Familiarize yourself with the accumulated literature, bring in speakers, or ask a professional who is openly gay or lesbian (from within or from outside your school) to discuss gay and lesbian issues with colleagues. Work against discriminatory practices that make it necessary for gays and lesbians to hide.

- Use gender-neutral language. If you use language that assumes a person is heterosexual (e.g., inquiring about a woman's boyfriend or husband), a gay or lesbian client may not feel that you are knowledgeable about their orientation and therefore, may not share valuable information with you. The use of words and terms such as "partner" or "someone special in your life" are appropriate, gender neutral, assumption free and important to use.

- Use the words "gay," "lesbian" or "bisexual" in an appropriate context when talking with clients about diversity. As social workers, we listen to many different groups of people (e.g., Latino, African-American, Asian-American, developmentally disabled). We must be inclusive and also mention people who are gay, lesbian, and bisexual. These words are important and signal your students and parents that you are open to discuss these issues with them.

- Have literature and other visible signs in the classroom or in your office that speak to creating a gay- and lesbian-affirming environment. Magazines, pamphlets, and posters with the words "gay" or "lesbian" printed on them let students and families know that you are sensitized and that your office or the school is a safe place. If you are interested in obtaining gay- and lesbian-affirming posters, you can call GLAD, San Francisco, CA, (415) 861-2244. There is also a Gay and Lesbian Help Line in Minneapolis, MN. The tool-free number for Minnesota, North Dakota, South Dakota, Iowa, Wisconsin, or Nebraska is 800-800-0907. If outside these states you may call the help line at (612) 822-8661.

- If a student or parent discloses to you that he or she is gay or lesbian, talk about it! Do not just move on. Talk about what it means for this student or parent to be a gay man or a lesbian. Process the feelings and assure the individual that you will respect their confidentiality.

- Do not confuse or equate transsexuality or transvestism with homosexuality. Be aware that these individuals are also members of sexual minority communities and may require services to meet their particular needs.

- If you are a gay or lesbian educator, come out! Visibility is powerful. Although gay and lesbian young people and their parents need role models, gay and lesbian people who are "out" should avoid becoming the "gay expert" in the school because having an expert tends to absolve others from becoming knowledgeable about gay and lesbian issues and exonerates systems from fully implementing the changes necessary for creating safe environments. If you are a heterosexual educator, you must also "come out" in openly supporting gay and lesbian colleagues, students, and parents.

Conclusion

Although the issue of sexual orientation frequently is framed as a "behavior" that is objectionable to some, disclosure of one's sexual orientation is the real challenge to society. As long as gays and lesbians neither name it nor claim it, everyone can pretend that they do not exist. Hartman (1993) wrote: "There is nothing more oppressive than denying another's reality. There is no better way to subjugate human beings than to silence them" (p. 245). Schools must recognize how oppression hurts all of everyone!

An understanding of the impact of societal stigmatization on gay and lesbian individuals and their families is crucial to recognizing and responding to the needs of this population. Effecting changes in attitudes and beliefs that lead to creating affirming environments and providing competent practice with gay and lesbian adolescents and their families requires education, training, and self-exploration on both individual and institutional levels. The development of practice competence and the creation of safe environments in this area is one positive step toward the establishment of appropriate gay- and lesbian-affirming educational services to address the needs of these young people and their families.

References

Borhek, M. V. (1988). Helping gay and lesbian adolescents and their families: A mother's perspective. *Journal of Adolescent Health Care, 9*(2), 123-128.

Borhek, M. V. (1983). *Coming out to parents.* New York: Pilgrim Press.

Commonwealth of Massachusetts Governor's Commission on Gay and Lesbian Youth. (1993). *Making schools safe for gay and lesbian youth: Breaking the silence in schools and in families.* Boston: Author.

Dew, R. F. (1994). *The family heart: A memoir of when our son came out.* Reading, MA: Addison-Wesley.

de Young, M. (1982). *The sexual victimization of children.* Jefferson, NC: McFarland.

Due, L. (1995). *Joining the tribe: Growing up gay and lesbian in the '90s.* New York: Anchor Books.

Fairchild, B., & Hayward, N. (1989). *Now that you know: What every parent should know about homosexuality.* New York: Harcourt Brace Jovanovich.

Germain, C. B. (1979). Ecology and social work. In C. B. Germain (Ed.), *Social work practice: People and environments* (pp. 1-22). New York: Columbia University Press.

Germain, C. B. (1991). *Human behavior and the social environment.* New York: Columbia University Press.

Germain, C., & Gitterman, A. (1980). *The life model of social work practice.* New York: Columbia University Press.

Gonsiorek, J. C. (1988). Mental health issues of gay and lesbian adolescents. *Journal of Adolescent Health Care, 9*(2), 114-122.

Griffin, C., Wirth, M. J., & Wirth, A. G. (1986). *Beyond acceptance.* Englewood Cliffs, NJ: Prentice-Hall.

Groth, A. N. (1978). Patterns of sexual assault against children and adolescents. In A. W. Burgess, A. N. Groth, L. L. Holmstrom, & S. M. Sgroi (Eds.), *Sexual assault of children and adolescents* (pp. 3-24). Lexington, MA: Lexington Books.

Groth, A. N., & Birnbaum, H. J. (1978). Adult sexual orientation and attraction to underage persons. *Archives of Sexual Behavior, 7*(3), 175-181.

Harbeck, K. M. (1993). Invisible no more: Addressing the needs of gay, lesbian, and bisexual youth and their advocates. *High School Journal, 77*(1-2), 169-176.

Hartman, A. (1993). Out of the closet: Revolution and backlash. *Social Work, 38*(3), 245-245, 360.

Hunter, J., & Schaecher, R. (1987). Stresses on lesbian and gay adolescents in schools. *Social Work in Education, 9*(3), 180-188.

Hunter, J., & Schaecher, R. (1990). Lesbian and gay youth. In M. J. Rotherram-Borus, J. Bradley, & N. Obolensky (Eds.), *Planning to live — Evaluating and treating suicidal teens in community settings* (pp. 297-316). Norman: University of Oklahoma Press.

Jennings, K. (1994a). *Becoming visible: A reader in gay and lesbian history for high school and college students.* Boston: Alyson.

Jennings, K. (1994b). *One teacher in ten.* Boston: Alyson.

Krysiak, G. J. (1987). Needs of gay students for acceptance and support. *The Education Digest, 53*(4), 44-47.

Mallon, G. P. (1992). Gay and no place to go: Assessing the needs of gay and lesbian adolescents in out-of-home care settings. *Child Welfare, 71*(6), 547-556.

Mallon, G. P. (1994). *We don't exactly get the welcome wagon: The experience of gay and lesbian adolescents in North America's child welfare systems.* New York: Columbia University Press.

Martin, A. D. (1982). Learning to hide: The socialization of the gay adolescent. In S. C. Feinstein, J. G. Looney, A. Schartzberg, & A. Sorosky, (Eds.), *Adolescent psychiatry: Developmental and clinical studies,* (Vol. 10., pp. 52-65) Chicago: University of Chicago Press.

Newton, D. E. (1978). Homosexual behavior and child molestation: A review of the evidence. *Adolescence, 13*(49), 205-215.

Norris, W. P. (1992). Liberal attitudes and homophobic acts: The paradoxes of homosexual experiences in a liberal institution. In K. M. Harbeck (Ed.), *Coming out of the classroom closet* (pp. 81-120). New York: Harington Park Press.

Parents & Friends of Lesbians and Gays, Inc. (1990). *Why is my child gay?* Washington, DC: Author.

Powell, R. E. (1987). Homosexual behavior and the school counselor. *School Counselor, 34*(3), 202-208.

Remafedi, G. (1985). Adolescent homosexuality: Issues for pediatricians. *Clinical Pediatrics, 24*(9), 481-485.

Remafedi, G. (1987a). Adolescent homosexuality: Psychosocial and implications. *Pediatrics, 79,* 331-337.

Remafedi, G. (1987b). Male homosexuality: The adolescent's perspective. *Pediatrics, 79,* 326-330.

Reynolds, A. L., & Koski, M. J. (1993). Lesbian, gay, and bisexual teens and the school counselor: Building alliances. *High School Journal, 77*(1-2), 88-94.

Rofes, E. R. (1989). Opening up the classroom closet: Responding to the educational needs of gay and lesbian youth. *Harvard Educational Review, 59*(4), 444-453.

Saperstein, S. (1981). Lesbian and gay adolescents: The need for family support. *Catalyst, 3-4*(12), 61-69.

Savin-Williams, R. C. (1989). Parental influences on the self-esteem of gay and lesbian youths: A reflective appraisals models. In G. Herdt (Ed.), *Gay and lesbian youth* (pp. 93-110). New York: Harrington Park Press.

Savin-Williams, R. C. (1994). Verbal and physical abuse as stressors in the lives of lesbian, gay male and bisexual youths: Associations with school problems, running away, substance abuse, prostitution, suicide. *Journal of Consulting and Clinical Practice, 62,* 261-269.

Savin-Williams, R. C. (1995). Lesbian, gay male, and bisexual adolescents. In A. R. D'Augelli & C. J. Patterson, (Eds.), *Lesbian, gay and bisexual identities over the lifespan: Psychological perspectives* (pp. 165-189). New York: Oxford University Press.

Savin-Williams, R. C., & Rodriguez, R. G. (1993). A developmental clinical perspective on lesbian, gay male and bisexual youth. In T. P. Gullotta, G. R. Adams, & R. Montemayor (Eds.), *Adolescent sexuality: Advances in adolescent development,* (Vol. 5, pp. 77-101). Newbury Park, CA: Sage.

Schneider, M. (1988). *Often invisible: Counseling gay and lesbian youth.* Toronto: Toronto Central Youth Services.

Sears, J. T. (1992). Educators, homosexuality, and homosexual students: Are personal feelings related to professional beliefs? In K. M. Harbeck (Ed.), *Coming out of the classroom closet* (pp. 29-80). New York: Harington Park Press.

Shernoff, M. & Finnegan, D. (1991). Family treatment with chemically dependent gay men and lesbians. *Journal of Chemical Dependency, 4*(1) 121-135.

Strommen, E. F. (1989). "You're a what?". Family member reactions to the disclosure of homosexuality. *Journal of Homosexuality, 18*(1/2), 37-58.

Tartiagni, D. (1978). Counseling gays in a school setting. *School Counselor, 26,* 26-32.

Whitlock, M. (1989). *Bridges of respect.* Philadelphia: American Friends Service Committee.

Making a Difference:
A Call for Education and Action

Eileen Bardwell Raymond
State University of New York — Potsdam

Today, in American schools, there are many young people who find that they do not fit, who realize that who they are is not acceptable in their families, schools, and communities. They feel if they are to survive they must hide or suppress their growing sexual feelings. These are youth who are gay, lesbian, or bisexual. In some schools, there are teachers who fear for their jobs because they believe that if anyone knew they were gay or lesbian, they would be fired or at least harassed. Like their younger counterparts, their invisibility deprives young people of role models necessary to understand the full range of possibilities in being human. Fortunately, there are other teachers, both gay and straight, who advocate for safe schools and social justice, who daily confront the forces of oppression in the form of homophobia and heterosexism. There are also young people who are confused and hurt by homophobic jokes and slurs because they have good friends or parents or other family members who are gay, lesbian, or bisexual. There are other groups of teens, both gay and straight, who form Gay-Straight Alliances to combat homophobia.

In every community, some young people live in social isolation, drop out of school, develop feelings of depression and lowered self-esteem, and attempt or complete suicide solely because they see no place for themselves in the human family because their primary affectional, erotic, and romantic attachments are with members of their own gender (Remafedi, 1994). Other youth who are gay and lesbian, those Joyce Hunter has called the "resilient kids," manage to navigate their teen years and develop a strong sense of self-worth.

What makes the difference? Attendees at this symposium addressed these issues through a series of keynote and small-group discussions. One outcome was the recognition of the need for information and action in schools and communities across the country.

Understanding the Issues Related to Providing Services to Adolescents Who Are Gay, Lesbian, or Bisexual

Central to the question of how to provide services to sexual minority youth is the issue of finding them. Many teachers, administrators, and parents believe that there are no youth in their student body who are gay, lesbian, or bisexual, that this "problem" pertains only to certain urban areas like San Francisco and New York City. This clearly is not true because a number of survey studies, reported by Wayne Pawlowski in his keynote address, repeatedly have confirmed that a finite percentage (varying from 1% to 10%) of the population has a homosexual orientation.

The challenge to find sexual minority youth is compounded by the developmental nature of sexual orientation, with children and youth gradually becoming aware of their feelings and attractions. Many will not become fully aware of their sexual identities until their twenties. By the time young people experience their first erotic feelings as young teens, society as a whole has communicated the values and attitudes that comprise heterosexism and homophobia; they already know that those feelings are something to hide, to be ashamed of, to resist.

Instead of asking "How do we find them to help them?" one might more appropriately ask "How do we allow them to find us?" As Gerald Mallon indicated in his keynote address, "The only real way to tell if a teen is gay, lesbian, or bisexual is for him or her to tell you." As the discussion group on whom this chapter is based pursued this question, it became apparent that there are many barriers to creating a climate where questioning youth who are gay, lesbian, or bisexual can find support they desperately need, to allow them to "tell us." Among the obstacles are (a) our personal discomfort with discussing issues of sexuality; (b) lack of information about sexuality and homosexuality among teachers, counselors, coaches, and social workers; (c) resistance from administrators and other teachers; and (d) the current political climate that has had a chilling effect on all aspects of sexuality education. The group voiced concern that any attempt at outreach has to be done in an "acceptable" way because of the fear of "passionate resistance" from those who wish to see that heterosexism and homophobia remain as the dominant value system.

Some participants stated the belief that gay or lesbian teens can spot the teachers who are sympathetic or supportive and that even as young people they have a developed sense of radar, or "gay-dar." Others voiced the concern that society cannot count on support being found by a gay, lesbian, or questioning teen. Many young people learn quickly from societal messages and from their first attempt to make contact with a support person that homosexuality is one area with which many otherwise trustworthy adults are not comfortable. The grim statistics of depression and suicide among sexual minority youth testify to the fact that gay and lesbian teens survive at great cost and only by hiding, distancing, and struggling on their own because talking to a parent or teacher is too big a risk (Remafedi, 1994).

To counteract these forces, teachers and others who have regular contact with young people can take several important steps to end the isolation of adolescents who are gay, lesbian, bisexual, or questioning. Education is the first step. Building on the work being done in other areas of oppression and bias, schools must hold mandatory staff development training sessions for all faculty, with the aim of providing the information essential to create a safe learning environment for all students. School professionals need to send the message that approval or disapproval of a particular intimate behavior does not matter; it only matters that schools are physically and psychologically safe places for all students. Staff training must focus on the issue of relationships. For too long, discussion about sexuality and sexual orientation has focused only on the sexual acts. Broadening the focus to include the development of affectional, erotic, and romantic orientations in the context of relationships will be more useful in establishing a context for this work.

Sexuality education for teens is a second area for work. Currently, the only place homosexuality is mentioned is in AIDS education, a potentially dangerous association for youth who are gay or straight. Students who are gay hear the message that their very identity is associated with death. Their heterosexual peers hear that AIDS is a gay issue, not something to worry about. Homosexuality should be included in all sexuality curricula as a normal variant on sexual identity. It is particularly important that sexuality education for students with disabilities contains in-

formation about the full range of sexual expression. Having a disability does not make a young person heterosexual or homosexual. Sexuality education should be provided by staff who are comfortable with all aspects of sexual identity and who can provide accurate and complete information. When students hear their teachers using the words gay and lesbian easily, fear breaks down. Sexual minority teens are more likely to see those teachers as safe allies.

The report from the Massachusetts Governor's Commission on Gay and Lesbian Youth (1993) stresses the need to make schools safe places for youth who are gay and lesbian.

School staff can give substance to these recommendations by mounting a "safe space" campaign. Faculty at a number of schools and colleges nationwide have voluntarily posted a symbol (e.g., pink triangle, rainbow flag, or other special sign) that indicates to all that this classroom or office is a safe space, where bigotry and oppression have no place. These teachers go further by addressing forcefully any stereotypic language they hear and by themselves using language sensitive to their diverse student body (e.g., using *partner* instead of *boyfriend* or *girlfriend*).

Teachers are of necessity the frontline of support. They see students daily and often build significant trust relationships with them. Initially, students are more likely to approach a teacher or coach than they are to seek out a guidance counselor who is seen as having other functions like college placement or solving major psychological problems. It is important to involve all teachers, gay or straight, in this work. Straight allies can often make the point for safety far better than the openly gay or lesbian staff person, whose motives are often viewed with suspicion. The effectiveness of PFLAG (Parents, Families, and Friends of Lesbians and Gays) illustrates how powerful straight allies can be in promoting social justice.

Finally, if school professionals are to help students who are questioning and in need of support during the process of developing into the adults they will be, they must help students find them. That means schools must change the climate of silence and fear that surrounds minority sexual orientations. School must be a safe place for every student. When our actions speak that message, the students will find us.

Examining Best Educational Practices: Incorporating the Needs of Adolescents Within School Goals

A major concern among this group's discussion participants was the sense of not having enough accurate information, of not knowing how to respond to questions and comments from students. It is clear that competence in the basic terminology is an essential place to start. Teachers and others who work with youth must be clear about what all the terms mean, and they must be sure that they and the students mean the same thing by the words that are being used.

Teachers can learn how to counsel in a nondirective but supportive way those students who come to them. The fact that a youngster is questioning does not presume that he or she will ultimately develop an exclusively homosexual identity. As Wayne Pawlowski reported (see his chapter, this volume), development of a sexual identity is a long process, often continuing into late adolescence or young adulthood. The helpful adult will be one who can assist teens in asking themselves the questions that will keep them exploring and feeling supported. The manual developed for use in Project 10 in Los Angeles (Friends of Project 10, 1989) offers specific guidelines for handling self-disclosure and questions from teens.

Building alliances of all kinds is essential. Allies among heterosexual faculty can be most effective when they work with teachers who are openly gay and lesbian. It is neither fair nor productive to expect that the staff who are gay and lesbian can effect change without support. The Gay, Lesbian, and Straight Teachers Network (GLSTN), has been working for over 5 years to build anti-homophobia alliances and currently has a national membership of over 1,000 gay and straight members.

Gay-Straight Alliances (GSAs) for students are becoming more common as well, particularly in Massachusetts where the Governor's Commission (1993) called for their establishment in all schools. GSAs are established to combat homophobia wherever it appears and to say to all students, "You have worth and dignity, gay or straight." The GSAs are often led by co-advisors, one gay and one straight, a powerful model that deserves emulation. Finally, because colleges generally are seen as providing more liberal environments than public schools, this group's discussants voiced the hope that alliances with local college faculty will help provide resources for anti-homophobia work.

In response to the question: "What would an ideal program look like?" there were a number of answers:

- The ideal "program" would have no walls and boundaries but rather would be infused throughout all aspects of the school program, directly linked into other programs and activities.

- It would include staff development training, possibly building on cultural diversity training models already in place. All oppression is interconnected. As Audre Lord, an African-American lesbian, wrote in 1983, "There is no hierarchy of oppressions." Resources exist in a number of places for conducting anti-oppression and anti-homophobia workshops (Alexander, 1990; Blumenfeld, 1992).

- The school and district should have strong written policies that declare zero tolerance for any hurtful or hate speech or slurs against anyone or any personal characteristic.

- The program would include a broad-based survey of the entire student body on all issues of diversity (e.g., ethnic, cultural, linguistic, class, religion, disability, gender, sexual orientation, appearance). A diversity survey conducted recently in a small rural high school revealed that there were small proportions of students willing to admit to racial prejudice, but that over half reported having negative feelings toward gays and lesbians, including a number of students who claimed to belong to a "gay-bashing club." Such a survey clearly indicates where the work needs to be done. In this case, the students' willingness to respond so openly with anti-gay feelings seems to indicate that they feel those responses are at least tacitly acceptable to the school staff.

- It would include a concerted effort to collect information on resources available for youth who are gay, lesbian, or questioning, including names of nonhomophobic counselors, community centers and support groups, hot lines, safe Internet list serves and chat lines, as well as books and periodicals. Those involved in anti-homophobia work must make librarians their allies. Books and periodicals on sexual minority issues should be part of every school's collection. Supportive teachers might want to purchase books for their personal lending library as well, to lend to students who are not ready to checkout a book from the library. Good choices are *The Journey Out: A Guide for and about Gay, Lesbian, and Bisexual Teens* (Pollack & Schwartz, 1995), *Two Teenagers in Twenty* (Heron, 1994); and *Becoming Visible* (Jennings, 1994a), a reader in gay history for teens.

Finally, any program must work to reduce the fear associated with this issue. What are the implications for serving young people and for establishing and maintaining safe and supportive environments when concerned adults are afraid to request funding and time off to attend a symposium like this because it has "those words" in the title?

Highlighting Realistic Actions That Could Result in More Accepting School Climates

The first step in creating a better climate for gay, lesbian, bisexual, or questioning teens as well as their teachers, is education and staff development training. This recommendation immediately raises the question, "Who will advocate for this with the administration and staff?" How can an individual get rid of the fear of the stigma that will follow one's open advocacy for sexual minority youth?

Jennings (1994b) and Woog (1993) present many firsthand stories of professionals, schools, and programs that address the issue of creating safe environments that are conducive to social adjustment of students and adults. In *One Teacher in Ten* , Jennings (1994a) shares the life experiences of gay and lesbian teachers in their own voices. It is essential that these stories be heard by all teachers and administrators, gay or straight, so that the scope of the impact of homophobia and heterosexism can be appreciated and dealt with. Woog presents stories of hope and courage as he describes the personal triumphs of individuals, as well as the successes of programs across the country. These models can provide the impetus for change in any school.

Why must schools change? Why exert the effort? The answers are simple. Homophobia hurts us all (Blumenfeld, 1992). When an individual fears being branded as "gay" for advocating for simple justice, homophobia hurts everyone. When a teacher shies away from supporting young people who are making this difficult journey without the usual social supports because he or she is afraid of the charge of "recruiting" or "turning them gay," homophobia hurts everyone. When an administrator fails to address a homophobic slur, it hurts everyone. Education professionals fail youth who are gay, lesbian, bisexual, and questioning; fail their straight friends; fail students who have parents or family members who are gay or lesbian; and fail their professional peers who are gay, lesbian, and bisexual. Homophobia hurts us all.

Establishing venues for informal conversation about life issues with supportive adults (e.g., rap rooms after school, community youth groups, and drop-in centers) may be a way for staff to create a climate where these issues can be raised. Schools and community groups can establish youth groups along the model of the Horizons program in Chicago (Herdt & Boxer, 1993) and the GSAs in Massachusetts. Such programs allow young people to explore their place in this social world in the company of others who understand and support them. Guidelines for adult advisors ensure that the highest ethical standards for youth work are upheld. As one of the teens involved in establishing a GSA reported in the final panel session, these groups are a vehicle for fighting homophobia and for helping young people advocate for justice and human rights. Being an advocate for yourself and for others effectively raises self-esteem and creates a sense of empowerment.

The Council for Children with Behavioral Disorders (CCBD) can assist in this work by regularly publishing reports on research about sexual orientation issues, on successful support programs, and on anti-homophobia work. Discussion in the professional literature will assist in making progress on behalf of the rights of individuals who are gay, lesbian, and bisexual. With a constant flow of information about the cost of homophobia and about programs that have been effective in other places, educators will be enabled to achieve needed societal change and also support those who are involved in this work. Silence and lack of information works against education professionals and the youngstèrs they serve.

Conclusion

We live in a society where heterosexism is culturally entrenched and where lack of information leads to discomfort when issues of sexual orientation are raised. Young people who are gay, lesbian, or bisexual are growing up in a climate that devalues who they are. Rather than risk the social cost of disclosure, they learn to hide, to "pass." Our task is to create an environment where all young people can grow up with the opportunities to learn the social skills relevant to their personal sexual identities.

Education and sharing of information are the keys to eliminating homophobia and heterosexism as a source of psychological pain and loss of human potential. Teenagers must be educated about the continuum of sexual identities and provided with appropriate sexuality education so that they can make responsible choices about their sexual behaviors. School professionals must be educated to appreciate the complex nature of the development of sexual identity and their role in facilitating the development of the youth in their charge. Communities must be educated so that societal acceptance of all young people can be achieved. Above all, a commitment to safe schools must prevail. Every youngster has a right to an education in a safe place; at present, too many teens are being deprived of that right to safety. Our fears must not keep us silent. Our fears must not keep us from making schools safe.

References

Alexander, S. W. (1990). *The welcoming congregation*. Boston: Unitarian Universalist Association.

Blumenfeld, W. (Ed.). (1992). *Homophobia: How we all pay the price*. Boston: Beacon.

Commonwealth of Massachusetts Governor's Commission on Gay and Lesbian Youth. (1993). *Making schools safe for gay and lesbian youth: Breaking the silence in schools and families* (Publication No. 17296-60-500-2/93-C.R.). Boston, MA: Author.

Friends of Project 10. (1989). *Project 10 Handbook: Addressing lesbian and gay issues in our schools: A resource directory for teachers, guidance counselors, parents and school-based adolescent care providers.* Los Angeles: Author. Available from Virginia Uribe, 7850 Melrose Avenue, Los Angeles, CA 90046.

Herdt, G., & Boxer, A. (1993). *Children of Horizons: How gay and lesbian teens are leading a new way out of the closet.* Boston: Beacon.

Heron, A. (Ed.). (1994). *Two teenagers in twenty.* Boston: Alyson.

Jennings, K. (Ed.). (1994a). *Becoming visible.* Boston: Alyson.

Jennings, K. (Ed.). (1994b). *One teacher in ten.* Boston: Alyson.

Lord, A. (Ed.). (1983). *Homophobia and education.* New York: Council on Interracial Books for Children.

Pollack, R., & Schwartz, C. (1995). *The journey out: A guide for and about gay, lesbian, and bisexual teens.* New York: Puffin Books (Penguin).

Remafedi, G. (Ed.). (1994). *Death by denial: Studies of gay and lesbian youth suicide.* Boston: Alyson.[1]

Woog, D. (1993). *School's out: The impact of gay and lesbian issues on American schools.* Boston: Alyson.

---

[1] Remafedi (1994) contains the complete text of Paul Gibson's study on gay male and lesbian youth suicide that was included in the U. S. Department of Health and Human Services Task Force Report on Youth Suicide in 1988. It also contains the full text of Massachusetts Governor's Commission on Gay and Lesbian Youth Education Report, *Making Schools Safe for Gay and Lesbian Youth.* The Education Report is also available in microfiche format, ERIC Document No. ED 367 923, as well as from the Governor's Commission offices.

Youth and Homosexuality

Ann Thompson Cook
Author, Educator, and Speaker on Topics
Related to Sexuality, Gender, and Reproductive Health
Washington, DC

Wayne Pawlowski
Director of Training Planned Parenthood of Metro DC
Washington, DC

Implications of Sexual Diversity Throughout Childhood

Some youth are lesbian or gay. Some youth are labeled lesbian or gay by others, whether they are or not. Some youth have lesbian or gay parents, siblings, or other relatives. All these young people suffer because of the stigma and prejudices surrounding homosexuality. Even more young people—including heterosexual youth—make important life decisions based on stigma, prejudice, and rampant misinformation, rather than on what is healthy and right for them.

Many adults continue to believe, erroneously, that homosexuality is learned or chosen. In fact, gay, lesbian, and bisexual people from every walk of life, religion, nationality, and racial background report that they knew at an early age—often as young as six or seven—that they were somehow different. Later, they realized that the difference had to do with their attraction to people of the same gender. Some come to this realization in their late teens or even later, but many young people realize they are lesbian, gay, or bisexual as early as junior high.

Currently, these young people are at high risk for serious social and emotional problems including alcohol and other drug abuse, teen pregnancy, drop-ping out of school, HIV/AIDS infection, and suicide. These youth are not at high risk because they are lesbian or gay; their distress is a direct result of the hatred and prejudice that surround them.

Much of the negativity about homosexuality and youth is based on misinformation about sexuality and sexual development. In this paper, we address two questions: "What do we know about sexuality, including homosexuality?" and "Given what is known, what needs to change?" We seek to explain important distinctions — too often blurred — among gender, gender role, gender identity, sexual attitudes and values, sexual orientation, and sexual behavior. In other words, we address these questions:

- How do we expect females and males to act and where do we get those expectations?

- What attitudes do we hold about sexuality and how did we develop them?

- To whom do we feel attracted and how do we recognize those attractions?

- What do we let other people know about ourselves as females and males?

- How do we behave, sexually?

- How accurate and complete is our information about sexuality?

This article was originally published as Issue Paper #3 of the Respect All Youth Project, Federation of Parents and Friends of Lesbians and Gays. The article is reprinted with permission from Parents, Families, and Friends of Lesbians and Gays.

Next, we discuss what difference information about sexuality makes to children as they grow up. As we will show, misinformation is hardly benign; it creates serious obstacles for all children in their efforts to learn about and affirm themselves.

Finally, we recommend ways that schools, youth agencies, religious congregations, and families can make their own settings more hospitable to all children who are trying to answer the question, "Who am I?"

Is It a Boy or a Girl?

Let's begin with the most basic concept: gender. Judging from the first question we ask at the birth of nearly every baby, gender seems to be the most fundamental aspect of our sexuality. Nearly everyone agrees that gender is a simple matter: either you're male or you're female.

But it is not always that simple. Consider, for example, the fact that every fetus starts out as a female. It is only after six weeks of development that those with the Y chromosome begin to differentiate as males. That differentiation, however, doesn't always proceed smoothly. In some babies genitals are ambiguous; there is some variation. It may be something simple like the clitoris being enlarged or the penis being small. Or it may be more obvious, as in the case of babies who appear to have both a penis and a vaginal opening.

What is done about such cases? After checking the baby's chromosomes and talking to the parents, the physician usually "corrects" the baby surgically according to the more dominant sex organs (not necessarily according to the chromosomes). That means that some people physically look female but are carrying XY (male) chromosomes, and some people look male but have the XX (female) chromosomes. And some people have even *more* complex chromosome combinations. Thus, even the simple business of being male and female is not as simple as it seems. And many other sexuality issues—such as gender roles, attitudes, and values—are just as complex.

Who Gets to Do What?

Children begin acquiring gender roles almost as early as they learn whether their "package" is male or female. The culture in which they live tells them, in both subtle and obvious ways, which things, given their package, they can and should do and which things they cannot and should not do. Children learn such expectations directly though instruction—"little girls (boys) don't do that"—and indirectly, through their powerful ability to observe other people's behavior. They watch those with the same package and those with the other package and try to behave accordingly. If you spend some time on an elementary school playground, you can tell that children pick up one particular gender role expectation very early: not to act "gay" (the words may be "sissy," "faggot," or "lezzie"), which really means not to act "like the other sex." This playground rule demonstrates the confusion of *gender role* with *sexual orientation*, a topic we will discuss later.

Such admonitions restrict many children. Young boys often are discouraged from exploring inclinations they may have toward "feminine" activities such as dancing, the arts, and music or toward "feminine" traits such as sensitivity. Young girls often end up pretending not to be "too strong" or "too smart," especially in "male" domains such as science and math. Think of the impact such restrictions have on personality development, relationships, and economics.

What Do We Believe?

In addition to what society expects, as individuals we have our own feelings about being male or female, our own beliefs about what is appropriate for us to do (or what we "should" do), and our own attitudes about various sexual acts. Those feelings, beliefs, and attitudes (our values) don't arise in a vacuum. Each of us has to make sense of the multiple and competing attitudes and values expressed in our families, in the prevailing culture, and in a wide variety of subcultures based on racial/ethnic identity, geographical location, socioeconomic standing, religious affiliation, and so on. Rarely do our values as individuals match exactly those of our families, our religious or ethnic heritage, or any other single source of influence.

Although as adults we often are not aware of teaching sexual attitudes and values, children are astute in picking them up in minute detail. At a very young age, for example, they discover that when they touch different parts of their bodies—elbows, toes, genitals—they get different reactions from adults. They learn that some parts are described with specific words—ear, shoulder, knee. Other parts are described with countless euphemisms—"down there," "wee-wee," "thing." Or, these body parts, may be surrounded by silence and not described at all; that silence speaks loudly about attitudes.

Children acquire a lot of information about values and sexuality in their first several years of life. Yet ironically, adults often talk as though teaching about sexuality, even as late as junior or senior high, will somehow imprint dangerous information and ideas on individuals without values. In reality, children already know what is out there, whether or not they can articulate it clearly. By the time they reach early adolescence, children have been deeply enculturated in the sexual attitudes and values of their family, the larger culture, and their particular subcultures.

Why are attitudes and values important? Because they operate more powerfully than any other factor in how we experience our sexuality and sexual behavior. For example, suppose one person thinks a particular sexual act is the most wonderful, beautiful expression of love possible, but another person thinks it is degrading, disgusting, and horrible. Now suppose these two people engage in that behavior together. Wouldn't they experience the same act at the same moment in entirely different ways? Their experience—enjoyment or disgust—would be based not on the act itself, but on their *attitudes* toward the act.

Similarly, attitudes toward lesbian and gay people powerfully influence youth. For example, in spite of evidence to the contrary, many people fear that gay or lesbian teachers, clergy, or youth workers will serve as "role models" and entice children into homosexuality. This fear implies that an individual third grade teacher who happens to be lesbian or gay could be so powerful an influence as to override years of heterosexual role modeling. At the least, it suggests that homosexuality is much more desirable or powerful than heterosexuality.

Strawberry or Chocolate: The Real Choices

In addition to gender, gender roles, and attitudes, another critical dimension of how we experience our sexuality is sexual orientation. First, notice our deliberate use of the word "orientation" rather than "preference." When people say, "I prefer strawberry ice cream to chocolate ice cream," chances are that if there is not strawberry, they'll be happy eating chocolate. Sexual *orientation* is an entirely different issue. If a young person is attracted to another young person, the choice is not whether or not to feel the attraction. The choice is *whether* and *how* to act on those feelings of attraction.

Many children develop sexual attraction toward people of the other gender (heterosexuality), many toward the same gender (homosexuality), and many toward both genders (bisexuality). The distinction among these attractions is only in the object of the feelings, not in the quality or validity of the feelings. Whichever direction these attractions take, however, the young people don't ask for it; it's not something they choose. There simply comes a time when they become aware of who or what excited them physically and emotionally. They become aware that they want to get next to that someone or something, that there's a powerful pull.

Distinct Issues: Identity, Orientation, Behavior

At this point, we want to make distinctions among four issues in sexual development:

- *Gender identity* is our perception of ourselves as male or female.
- *Sexual orientation* has to do with the object of our emerging emotional and physical attractions.
- *Sexual identity* has to do with how we label our orientation (heterosexual, homosexual, bisexual).
- *Sexual behavior* is what we "do" with our sexuality.

These distinctions are extremely important. There was a time when psychiatrists claimed to be "curing" homosexuals, but they had not distinguished among orientation, identity, and behavior. It's true that people who are predominantly homosexual can change their *behavior* by behaving heterosexually (and many do, to hide). They can change their *identity* by calling themselves heterosexual (or ex-gay). But no one has been successful in changing her or his basic *sexual orientation*—the direction of feelings of attraction. Indeed, turning this example around, we can see that many predominantly heterosexual people can, given particular circumstances, behave homosexually (and many do), but they would consider the idea of altering their predominant heterosexual orientation to be ridiculous.

It may sound as though we're saying orientation is fixed. For some people—both heterosexual and homosexual—it appears to be. For others, their understanding of their personal sexual orientation seems to evolve with new discoveries and experiences over a lifetime.

Labeling Identity: How Do We Know?

Moving from the *experience* of sexual orientation to the *labeling* of sexual identity, then, becomes extremely complex. A person who is sexually attracted to the other gender and engages in sexual behavior only with the other gender generally is labeled *heterosexual* in our culture. A person who is attracted to the same gender and engages only in same-gender sexual behavior is labeled *homosexual*.

But to underscore the complexity of labeling, consider the young woman who is strongly attracted to other women but marries a man and has children. What label do we apply? Do we identify her as heterosexual on the basis of her heterosexual behavior? Homosexual on the basis of her feelings? Bisexual? Does she label herself lesbian while continuing to behave heterosexually? And what if she confides her feelings to a friend who then gossips about her? Does she consider herself heterosexual, based on her relationship with her husband, while the neighborhood now labels her lesbian? Or what about people who are attracted to people of the other gender but are confined to a same-gender community (such as prison) and for a year or two have sexual relations only with people of the same gender? Their *behavior* is unquestionably homosexual. But when they return to the general society and have access to people of the other gender, they revert to having sexual relations with them. How do we label them? Do we go by their feelings? By their past behavior? By their current behavior? Should we be in the business of labeling at all? Only individuals can really know what their feelings and experiences mean to them.

Now if sexual identity has to do with labeling ourselves according to our orientation (the object of our affection) and our behavior (what we do), how do we understand *transsexuals*, people who believe they are trapped in a body of the wrong gender? Using the previous definitions, transsexualism is *not an issue of orientation*. Rather, it is an issue of gender identity—being anatomically female but feeling male, or being anatomically male but feeling female.

We have avoided using the pronouns "she" and "he." Again, the question of labeling: If a person is anatomically female and feels male, do we label that person according to the anatomy (she) or the feeling experience (he)?

We can begin to see how complex sexuality is and how confused the messages are about homosexuality, bisexuality, and heterosexuality. Frequently, we hear the stereotype that lesbians are women who want to be men, and gay men aren't "real" men. In addition to being factually incorrect, such stereotypes confuse issues of gender identity and sexual orientation—which, as we have shown, are really distinct issues.

In the Absence of Knowledge

Clearly, knowledge is an important component of sexuality, but there is the tragedy for most young people today: They move through their developmental process—identifying who they are, what they can do as males and females, how they feel about it, and whom they want to be with—before they even *begin* to get accurate information about sexuality. Thus, they often label themselves and each other in inappropriate or hurtful ways. This labeling makes growing up and sorting out feelings and experiences extremely confusing—not only to lesbian and gay youth, but also to other youth as well. Many teens avoid activities that might result in their being labeled:

I really enjoyed the ballet class we had in summer camp, but this fall the girls are calling me "ballet boy," so I'd better drop out and act cool.

Girls aren't supposed to be good at math, so I'd better hide my interest, if I want to be liked and get dates.

I like being a boy and I feel drawn toward some boys, but people say that gay men want to be women, and that's not me, so I couldn't be gay.

Yes, Children Are Sexual

Another misunderstanding about sexual development is that children become sexual when they reach puberty. We all know about the so-called "raging hormones" and growth spurts of early adolescence. But children are sexual long before then. Infant boys have erections. Infant girls lubricate vaginally. Nor does awareness of sexual orientation require the physical development of puberty. Many lesbian and gay people report having had sexual feelings toward others of the same gender early in elementary school, although they probably had not yet understood or labeled those feelings. *Being* sexual, of course, says nothing about behavior. Although by early adolescence, youngsters usually have a sense of who or what they want to get near (orientation), their awareness does not automatically translate into having genital sex (despite messages to the contrary in movies and TV).

Orientation Revisited

In spite of the fact that the major mental health associations dropped homosexuality from their list of mental disorders in the 1970s, many therapists continue to view sexual differences as "deviant" and try to "correct the problem" of sexual orientation—sometimes with extreme measures such as electroshock and aversion therapy. No matter how diligently researchers have tried to demonstrate causes of or cures for homosexuality, there is no evidence that it is an illness, that is caused by particular family patterns or experiences, or that it can be eliminated or changed. In fact, study after study has documented that homosexual persons experience the *same* variations of mental health and family backgrounds as are found among heterosexual persons.

In addition to the research on "causes" of sexual orientation, Alfred Kinsey's ground-breaking study during the 1940s yielded important information by asking people about their sexual *behavior* throughout the course of their lives. He developed the famous Kinsey Scale, which recognized for the first time that—behaviorally—most people are neither completely heterosexual nor completely homosexual, but somewhere in between. Based on the behaviors people reported to him, Kinsey concluded that a significant proportion of the United States population engages in same-gender behavior (Reinisch, 1990).

Since Kinsey reported his early findings, our understanding of sexual orientation has grown. Orientation is not simply behavior—"who did what with whom." Other factors—such as fantasies, affection, and gender identity—are equally, if not more, important.

Fantasies. People's fantasy lives (what they imagine or day dream) are particularly significant. To explain what we mean, we will give an example from our experience answering a community hotline. The example may be uncomfortably explicit, but it really happened, and it demonstrates how confusing these issues get for young people. The caller was a 15-year-old boy who said he was gay and wanted to know where to find the gay community. With some encouragement, the boy related the following incident: He had been at a party, gotten drunk, and passed out. When he regained consciousness, he was aware that someone was performing oral sex on him. All evening, he had been trying to get the attention of one particular girl, and he assumed, in his half-awake stupor, that the "someone" was that girl. Believing that he had finally won her over, he fully enjoyed the sexual experience. When he opened his eyes, however, he realized it was not the girl but a boy. His conclusion: "Since I enjoyed a sexual experience with another boy, I must be gay."

The incident did not mean he was gay, nor did it mean he was attracted to males. While his body was busy having an exclusively homosexual experience, his mind was fantasizing about an exclusively heterosexual experience. Clearly, fantasy is an essential consideration in determining the meaning of a sexual experience.

Affection. Affection is another key ingredient. Think of the people you know who have a sexual partner to whom they don't really feel close emotionally, but who have deep and close emotional bonds (friendships) with people who are not their sexual partners. This tells us that our affectional bonding may be with a variety of individuals and with people of both genders.

Gender identity. Now consider how truly complex the concept of orientation becomes with people who are transsexual. If a transsexual person who has a female package but a male gender identity has a sexual encounter with a male, what is the transsexual person's *orientation*? If we look at both packages (female and male), we would say heterosexual. If we look at gender identity (male and male), we would say homosexual. Clearly, the only person who knows for sure is the person having the experience.

The Effects of Stigmatization as Children Grow

Let us put aside the issue of sexuality and consider what this complex information has to do with growing up. First, what is required to move through puberty and adolescence into adulthood? As you know, adolescents change rapidly and dramatically in three areas: physical, intellectual, and psychosocial. Although the three areas of change are closely linked, physical and intellectual development proceed whether the young person wants them to or not. Psychosocial development, on the other hand, must take place within a social context, with the adolescent actively engaging in the process.

According to Erikson (1968), psychosocial development is the process of learning about oneself in relationship to peers and adults. As you read the following tasks in psychosocial development, consider how difficult it would be for lesbian and gay youth to move through them.

- *Identity*—Develop a strong, consistent sense of "who I am" that does not change dramatically from one context to the next.

- *Intimacy*—Develop a capacity for mature relationships, both sexual and emotional, with the same gender and with the other gender, with lovers as well as friends.

- *Integrity*—Develop a clear sense of what is right and wrong, including socially responsible attitudes and behaviors.

- *Psychological independence*—Develop a sufficiently strong sense of self to enable one to make decisions, to move through the world independently, and to assume adult roles, prerogatives, and responsibilities.

- *Physical independence*—Develop a capacity to provide for oneself (income, shelter, transportation, etc.).

The question arises—What happens to psychosocial development when an adolescent begins to discover feelings and attractions toward the same gender? Knowing our culture's abhorrence of all things homosexual, such youth often begin to distance themselves emotionally from other people. They don't want anyone to know what they're feeling, and so they shut others out. And who is shut out? Generally, the people who are most important in their development: family members, friends, teachers, clergy.

People who work with these youth report common threads, namely, the young people tend to deny the stigmatized role, feel intensely isolated, despise themselves, hide their true feelings from others, and live in fear of (or live with actual) rejection and violence (Martin, 1982).

- *Denial: "Not me!"* Because such youth often are not acquainted with healthy gay, lesbian, or bisexual individuals, they rely on the negative stereotypes they have been taught—that these people are sick, bad, immoral, and self-destructive. The discrepancy between these images and what a young person believes she or he is really like can be very confusing. It makes it difficult for the young people to understand the real feelings they are having, because they think, "I'm not like that!"

- *Isolation: "I'm so alone."* Many lesbian and gay youth speak of being different, believing no one else feels the way they feel. At a time when they want desperately to belong, they feel incredibly isolated.

- *Poor self-image "I'm no good."* Because these young people have heard societal judgments against what they feel, many conclude that, because they have these feelings, they must be worthless. ("If you really knew who I am, you would not love me.")

- *Hidden orientation: "I have to be so careful."* Again, gay and lesbian youth may wish to tell someone about their feelings, to discuss them. But they fear, often with good reason, that to do so would be to face rejection if not outright violence. Because most teens are still dependent on their families to meet their basic needs (housing, food, clothing), they may be particularly fearful of their families' judgments and reactions. Many youth are aware that their ticket to maintaining acceptance by peers and adults is to deceive them, to lie about what they're thinking and feeling, to pretend to think and feel "like everyone else." Thus, nothing they do can be spontaneous. Even when they appear to behave spontaneously, they are monitoring themselves so as not to give away their secret feelings. Some overcompensate for what they feel is their "defect" by excelling in school, sports, music, student government, or some other arena.

- *Fear of or actual rejection and violence "I'm not safe."* Boys and girls whose behavior or style does not fit rigid definitions of "appropriate" maleness or femaleness often are labeled as gay or lesbian, whether they are or not. Those who do "come out," as well as those who are labeled (whether lesbian/gay, or not), are often taunted, beaten, or driven from their homes, schools, religious groups, and communities.

Life-Threatening Consequences

Although available data are inadequate, some researchers and youth outreach workers suggest that nonheterosexual teens make up 30% or more of the young people who are living on the streets. They also represent a significant proportion of the teens at risk for dropping out (or being run out) of school, abusing alcohol and other drugs, running away, becoming pregnant, and attempting suicide.

Tragically, young women and young men (lesbian, gay, or straight) are under tremendous pressure to have heterosexual sex. Some are trying to "prove" they're not gay or lesbian ("I made a baby, so I can't be lesbian/gay!"). Some are exploring their feelings ("Are they real? Could I change?"). Whatever the motivation, many youth place themselves at risk for pregnancy, HIV/AIDS and other sexually transmitted diseases, and abusive relationships by engaging in sex.

Given societal condemnation, the first same-gender sexual experiences for many gay males are often anonymous encounters. They tend to happen in situations that are dangerous, degrading, and overwhelmingly sexual. Or they may occur in apparently safe and innocent places, but with high-risk activities. For example, a young man may have no idea whom he is with (or that the person may be infected with HIV/AIDS).

Growing up gay, lesbian, or bisexual in a culture that condemns homosexuality can stunt important psychosocial development in youth. Imagine how difficult it is for such youth to learn "who I am" in a social context, clarify their values through social interaction, experience themselves in intimate emotional and sexual relationships, and develop physical and emotional independence. Although some gay, lesbian, and bisexual youth are resilient, many go through adolescence feeling isolated and fearful and sustaining emotional distance.

For many people, it is only later, when they come out (at whatever age), that they work through these important adolescent tasks. Only then are they able to immerse themselves in the emotional/physical/social context that is so necessary for healthy psychosocial development.

Creating Hospitable Settings for All Children and Youth

Given what we know about sexuality and the effects of misinformation and stigma on children and youth, what should be done? Clearly, many changes are needed if society — especially organizations and institutions that care for, educate, and serve youth — is to prevent serious negative physical and mental health consequences of sexual diversity. Pretending that we simply can tell children and teens how to feel and how to behave is dangerous. They need information. Furthermore, they need settings that are safe and responsive to their concerns. They need help thinking through ways to prevent serious problems (such as HIV infection and pregnancy) in discussions that are relevant to the lives they are leading. Following is a brief list of essential changes.

First, break the silence. In everyday conversation, parents, teachers, and others who relate to children and adolescents can acknowledge and affirm diversity, even in the simplest changes beginning in early childhood. For example, in conversations about family life, a youth worker might say, "Some children have one parent, some have a mom and dad, some have two moms or two dads . . ."

A wonderful way to break the silence in schools and youth groups is to place in visible locations pamphlets, books, and posters that give information about lesbian, gay, and bisexual people and services.

Comprehensive education about sexuality (including sexual orientation) must begin in early childhood and must be geared to the questions and concerns of each age group. Such education should help children understand sexuality *in all its complexity*, rather than simply as something people "do" with their genitals. Following are examples of some basic messages:

- Just as individuals come in many shades of skin, eye, and hair color, families come in all sizes and orientations.

- People's sexual responses vary in many ways. One normal variation is in the object of one's emotional and sexual attractions; many people are attracted to the other gender, many to the same gender, many to both.

- Feelings, sexual responses, and objects of attraction are not "caught" like an illness, but are an integral part of a person, usually discovered rather than chosen.

- Throughout our lives, we can and do make decisions about how we behave, how we treat ourselves and other people.

Accurate information and carefully considered values are essential for young people as they make important decisions, to help them decide to behave in ways that are humane, healthy, and caring rather than insensitive and destructive.

Second, make it safe. Frequently, when youth experience sexually based harassment or name calling, they have no place to turn. Appealing to authority figures for help often makes matters worse. So they remain silent. Harassment or discrimination based on sexual orientation needs to be spelled out as unacceptable, just like any other harassment or discrimination. One way to do this is to amend human relations policies by adding sexual orientation to the list of protected categories, along with race, gender, physical capability, and so on. In addition, those in authority should promptly follow up on complaints and violations. Finally, knowing that many lesbian, gay, and bisexual youth remain silent and fail to seek help, people in authority should speak on their behalf and not tolerate harassment and abuse.

Another way to make it safe for youth is to make it safe for the lesbian, gay, and bisexual adults in their midst. Because healthy, normal lesbian, gay and bisexual teachers and youth workers have been fired in many localities when their orientation became known, most hide their identity. There are tens of thousands of healthy nonheterosexual persons working in schools, religious institutions, and youth agencies. If they were free to be as open about their orientation as are heterosexual staff, their very presence could alleviate great stress for lesbian, gay, and bisexual youth and would undercut much of the stigmatization and stereotyping surrounding sexual orientation. One way to accomplish this goal is to add sexual orientation to antidiscrimination language in personnel policies. The point is that we must create a learning environment in which all students (including lesbian, gay, and bisexual students) can thrive and grow without fear of harassment and discrimination and can learn about their culture and community.

Third, teach the grownups. Most educators and youth-serving professionals have undergone extensive training around issues related to the special concerns of youth. Most report, however, that they have had little or no training in sexuality, much less homosexuality; most are operating under their own biases, prevalent misconceptions, and misinformation. Ideally, all adults who work with youth would have specialized education in sexuality.

People in certain positions must have even more in-depth knowledge, especially: health, physical education, home economics, or science teachers (whoever is responsible for curricula dealing with health, sexually transmitted disease, and sexuality); mental health counselors; health care providers; clergy; and personnel running prevention programs for high-risk behaviors, including substance abuse, HIV/AIDS and other sexually transmitted diseases, pregnancy, school drop-out, and suicide.

Sexuality education should include the following objectives:

- Introduce up-to-date information about sexual development and sexual orientation.

- Clearly distinguish among sexual orientation, sexual behavior, and sexual identity.

- Recognize the profound negative impact of homophobia on the development and health of all adolescents.

- Reduce prejudice toward gay and lesbian youth and adults.

- Recognize the possibility of sexuality issues when students are involved in suicide attempts, dropping out of school, running away, pregnancy, and substance abuse (and thereby enhance the recovery process for these students).

- Introduce specific language changes to overcome exclusion (such as *date* rather than girl/boyfriend).
- Build skills to stop harassment.

Such training must occur over time. The Philadelphia School District offers a four-day in-service training for teachers, counselors, and administrators entitled "Equity in an Era of Diversity." One entire day is devoted to issues of heterosexism and homophobia and their impact on adolescents and the school environment. In Minneapolis/St. Paul, the University of Minnesota Youth and AIDS Project teaches school professionals about adolescent homosexuality and risk factors for lesbian and gay students in an effort to prevent HIV transmission, suicide, drug abuse, and dropping out of school.

Fourth, teach about the real world. Make sure that school curricula and other programs acknowledge famous lesbian and gay people (such as Bessie Smith and Walt Whitman) who have made important contributions in such areas as art, literature, music, science, history, medicine, and sports; include information about the oppression of gay and lesbian people throughout history, such as their persecution during the Holocaust; provide access to resources in the library on sexuality (including homosexuality), gay/lesbian history, and fiction with gay/lesbian protagonists.

Fifth, include parents. Most parents never consider the possibility that their own children, or their children's friends, may be lesbian, gay, or bisexual, or that other parents may be. Nevertheless, around 85% of American adults (and even more parents) consistently have supported the idea of schools' providing comprehensive information about sexuality to children and youth. Parents need such education as well—the same kind of education we recommend for teachers, counselors, clergy, administrators, and youth workers—preferably while their children are still young.

Sixth, support sexual minority youth. Regardless of other measures, sexual minority youth need avenues to air their concerns, both individually and among themselves. They also deserve opportunities to socialize freely in protected, non-erotic settings.
Numerous communities around the country have recognized lesbian and gay youth as a population with special unmet needs and have established community-based services. Some examples include the following:

- In Washington, DC, the Sexual Minority Youth Assistance League offers weekly opportunities for socialization and support.
- Members of the Indianapolis Youth Group run a toll-free hotline for teens who have questions and concerns about their sexuality, who may feel isolated in other communities, or who desperately need to talk with another young person like themselves.
- The Department of Recreation in Seattle offers Halloween dances for lesbian and gay youth, among other events.

Some schools are addressing the need as well.

- The San Francisco school system, requires each high school to designate at least one person who has volunteered to be available to students who have concerns about sexual orientation.
- Fairfax High School, with the full support of the Los Angeles Unified School District, has instituted Project Ten, which offers individual counseling, anonymous telephone counseling, and peer discussion groups for youth with sexual concerns.

Seventh, develop broad-based support. Efforts to implement any of these recommendations may be attacked by a small but well-organized, vocal, and often vicious group of people. The key to handling such controversy is to offer a support network before the controversy begins. Such support systems should include, among others, religious leaders, respected mental health professionals, parents, community agencies that serve at-risk youth, and city council and school board members.

A Bill of Rights for All Youth

In conclusion, we offer this bill of rights, proposed by Dr. Virginia Uribe, Director of Project Ten (adapted to apply beyond school settings). According to Dr. Uribe, every young person should be entitled to

- Schools and other youth programs free of verbal and physical harassment.
- An enforced standard of respect and dignity for all.
- Access to accurate information, free of negative judgment, delivered by trained adults who both inform and affirm all youth.
- Positive role models available in person, in school curricula, and in program implementation.
- Support programs that help them deal with the difficulties of adolescence and find their way to self-acceptance.

References

Donovan, P. A. (1989). *Risk and responsibility: Teaching sex education in America's schools today.* New York: Alan Guttmacher Institute.

Erickson, E. (1968). *Identity: Youth and crisis.* New York: W.W. Norton.

Martin, A.D. (1982). Learning to hide: The socialization of the gay adolescent. *Annals of the American Society for Adolescent Psychiatry 10,* 52-65.

Reinisch, J.M. (1990). *The Kinsey Institute new report on sex.* New York: St. Martin's Press.

Gay, Lesbian, and Bisexual Adolescents: Finding Them, Understanding Them, and Recognizing Their Potential

Joseph R. Ridky
Montgomery County Public Schools, Rockville, MD
and Chair, Task Force on Gay, Lesbian, and Bisexual Issues,
National Association of School Psychologists

Openly gay men and lesbian women have made their mark in almost every area of U.S. culture from college campuses to industry, and business to the arts, the military, and the church. However, for those who still think that homosexuals should stay in the closet, the typical American high school reflects that belief. Gay, lesbian, and bisexual (GLB) youth are in our schools, but they cannot risk to *come out*, as it would bring too much hardship on themselves and their families. These students feel terribly lonely.

But loneliness is not the only problem. In a 1994 study by the Montgomery County, Maryland Committee on Hate/Violence, a telephone survey of 635 randomly selected Montgomery County Public School's junior and senior high school students found that 53.1% of the respondents reported gays and lesbians as the group most discriminated against. Focus groups conducted in the fall of 1993 found that the types of discrimination included verbal taunts or "name calling," harassment and intimidation, and physical threats and attacks. When asked to rate the quality of the job their schools were doing to combat prejudice against gay people, 28.9% of students chose "Not very good at all." Indeed, only 11.1%, the lowest percentage category for this question, selected "A very good job" in response to the question.

Similarly, in Massachusetts, a survey designed by the Governor's Commission on Gay and Lesbian Youth was distributed to all students at Lincoln-Sudbury Regional High School in February of 1993. The survey included responses by 398 students. Students were asked the question, "Would you be upset or afraid if people thought you were gay, lesbian, or bisexual? Among the respondents, 60% said "yes," 22% did not know how they would feel, and only 18% said "no." A United States Senate report on youth suicide (U. S. Department of Health and Human Services, 1989) demonstrated that 45% of gay males and almost 20% of lesbians have experienced verbal abuse or physical assault in high school; about 28% of those students dropped out of school.

Understanding the Issues Related to Providing Services to Adolescents Who Are Gay, Lesbian, or Bisexual

There is enormous pressure to be accepted in high school. Therefore, students who are GLB keep their homosexuality hidden from their friends, family, and in many ways from themselves—they play the game. They date, go to dances and parties, sleep with the opposite sex to convince themselves that they are not gay, and generally stay invisible. Most adolescent gays and lesbians feel that they are the only one in their school. Anguish over whether others will find out their secret drives some GLB young people into depression and even attempted suicide. If homosexuality were more accepted in schools, some of this anguish would dissipate and, perhaps, so would be barriers to adopting a healthy homosexual lifestyle. For most students who are GLB, fears about *coming out* are warranted because most schools could easily then become a hostile environment for them. A court case currently in litigation in Wisconsin (Ashland District School System) demonstrates the violence that one child experienced for 5 years, violence which led to several failed attempts at suicide and eventually his leaving school altogether. Antigay violence by teenagers is widespread, as documented in multiple studies of lesbian and gays who suffer violence during their youth.

Because many ethnic groups have seized the "multicultural/discrimination spotlight" and because youths who are GLB are mostly invisible in schools, these individuals are excluded from multicultural task forces and GLB issues are not included in sensitivity training modules. More recently, cultural diversity is being celebrated in schools as one of America's greatest offerings. Every year there is a Black History Month or a celebration of Hispanic culture, but similar recognition is not afforded to the GLB community because society still does not recognize it as a "community." As an example, there are high schools in the United States named after Walt Whitman, but very few of the students in attendance know that he was a homosexual, nor is there any attempt by the school to discuss and educate the students about that fact. The same situation generally is not true for students who attend a school named after the well-known black American, Benjamin Bannaker. Diversity programs usually do not include sexual minority issues.

Many students who are GLB feel that their stress is exacerbated by the lack of positive role models. Although many educators in American schools are GLB, very few come out of the closet. Teachers are reluctant even to mention the subject in class. Books by gay authors may be read in class, and the teacher will never tell the students that the authors are (were) gay. Because of this, many students who are GLB are being denied a part of their culture. It is difficult to convince school administrators and educators that homosexuality is prevalent enough to warrant special attention. The fact is that parents, faculties, and most students find the subject extraordinarily threatening.

Examining Best Educational Practices: Incorporating the Needs of Gay, Lesbian, and Bisexual Adolescents Within School Goals

All students, including those who are GLB, need to know that when they enter a school building, everyone is protected against discrimination and there is equity for all. Schools need to be proactive in making certain that students can learn in an environment free of harassment and violence. Discrimination policies have to include sexual orientation; the silence must be broken regarding homosexuality and bisexuality. To attain this result, teachers, counselors, school psychologists, and school staff in general need to be trained in prejudice reduction, crisis intervention, and violence prevention.

Responsible teachers must take the lead by modeling appropriate behaviors that result in a school atmosphere free from discrimination and abuse. When abuse does occur, school administrators need to act swiftly to protect the victim and to send a message to the rest of the student body that this kind of behavior will not be tolerated. Ignoring these situations or justifying them (e.g., "Boys will be boys" or "If he or she did not act that way, this would not happen") is no longer acceptable.

School boards across the country also need to incorporate appropriate language and terminology into their human relations policies that set the standards for school staff to follow. Many professional associations and guilds have position statements and resolutions that support best practices for their members and GLB youth. However, these resolutions are very often difficult to implement in the school system when a professional is scared or feels threatened that those "appropriate" viewpoints and responses may just put his or her job in jeopardy.

Highlighting Realistic Actions That Could Result in More Accepting School Climates

According to reports at this symposium, there is now an increasing number of high schools that have officially recognized gay support and gay-straight alliance clubs. A teacher at this symposium reported that while teaching a course on "Homosexuality and the Law" in a Westchester County, New York school system, he found that many students who are GLB were meeting on their own, outside the school building. The local [teachers'] union president brought the issue to the Superintendent of Schools in order that the group could be officially recognized. They have now been meeting regularly since September of 1995. It was also reported that in many of New York City's private schools there now exists a Gay-Straight Alliance. Unfortunately, clubs such as these also have the potential to promote "gay bashing" because students become stigmatized when others see them entering these meetings. Having heterosexual teenagers involved in these support groups may be helpful, as it defuses the stigma that might be associated with one belonging to such a group if the group comprised only GLB students.

Some schools no longer are condoning name-calling (e.g., *faggot, dyke*). These offensive words need to be specifically banned in the school's behavior code. More enlightened schools appear to be providing books on the subject in easy-to-access areas of the school library. More teachers are leaving pertinent literature out and available for students to read. Some teachers have pasted small pink triangles on their classroom doors or offices (a sign of gay liberation stemming back to the pink cloth triangles that sexual-minority citizens had to wear during the Third Reich prior to their extermination in the death camps) letting students know that this is a place of understanding and safety.

Counseling is a critical element that must be made available to GLB youth. In major metropolitan areas where gay and lesbian community centers exist, youth programs with age-appropriate socialization activities are usually offered. However, most of these programs are for young people between the ages of 18 and 23. The support services are often not available for younger teens. Counseling for adults is also important. The myth that homosexuality is a lifestyle choice and the fear of recruitment into a GLB lifestyle is still very prevalent in discussions, especially by those who see sexual orientation as a choice that one could change if he or she wanted to do so. That nonsensical stance has got to be debunked by more responsible adults and professionals. The idea that one can change a person's sexual orientation has little scientific basis.

Another suggestion is that various groups such as counselors and staff from local youth sexual minority leagues; members of the Gay, Lesbian, Straight Teachers Network (GLSTN); and/or members of the local chapter of Parents and Friends of Gays and Lesbians (P-FLAG) can be invited into junior and senior high schools yearly to deliver workshops on the subject. In addition to the efforts of these outside support groups, the schools have to make broad-based efforts to reduce homophobia, including expanding the sexuality education programs in schools. Al-though many school districts indicate that they have sexuality education in their schools, many of these programs are inadequate. They need to include not just anatomy and physiology but comprehensive information on traditional and nontraditional sexual values, bisexuality, homosexuality, sexual health, intimacy, and sexual development. It is during these classes that issues pertaining to homophobia can be confronted directly, with time for class discussions. School counselors and school psychologists can support efforts to reduce homophobia because they are generally regarded as the *mental health expert* in a school building.

Conclusion

There is still much work to be done in order to create safe and nurturing environments for all youth. In these environments, youth find support, role models, accurate information, and guidance to enable them to develop into well adjusted adults who are free of stigma and discrimination.

References

Commonwealth of Massachusetts Governor's Commission on Gay and Lesbian Youth. (1993). *Making schools safe for gay and lesbian youth: Breaking the silence in schools and in families.* Boston: Author.

U. S. Department of Health and Human Services. (1989). *Task force report on youth suicide.* Washington, DC: Author.

New Directions for Lesbian, Gay, and Bisexual Youth:

Reflections on the Harvey Milk School

Joyce Hunter
HIV Center for Clinical and Behavioral Studies/
New York State Psychiatric Institute
Columbia University
New York City

Why An Alternative High School Program for Gay, Lesbian, and Bisexual Youth?

Few persons would disagree with the assertion that all students have a right to a high school education. For students who are gay, lesbian, or bisexual (GLB), public high schools have been a source of tremendous stress. For many students identified as GLB at school, this identification leads to harassment (both verbal and physical), while teachers and support staff often look the other way as these incidents occur. Not surprisingly, the school climate that emerges undermines the ability of these students to obtain an education, eventually leading many to drop out of school.

According to the literature, most young people come to the realization that they are gay or lesbian during their high school years. As the young person comes into awareness of homosexual feelings, he or she also becomes aware of being a member of a hated group. There is often confusion—confusion about gender roles and about life choices. Who are they going to share this information about themselves with, without fear of rejection by a family member or peers? These youngsters must learn to cope in a hostile climate and begin to develop coping skills—especially important is learning to hide. Hiding distorts the process of growing up and some of these young people have "hidden" behind a pregnancy or by having two relationships—one gay and one straight. Parents of these youngsters feel they do not know their own child, which exacerbates these young people's

feeling of being isolated. They want to meet people like themselves. Frequently, young women become partners because of loneliness. And when the relationship dissolves these young women are at risk for suicide—as many as 23% of them consider or attempt it.

Growing up and coming out—two processes at the same time—are especially difficult. Young gays and lesbians have little support for personal identity development; they are not prepared for their minority status. Although this discussion focuses on the problems of lesbian and gay youth, it is important to point out that the majority of these young people manage to develop coping skills and get on with their lives while in the process of hiding their sexual orientation.

The Harvey Milk High School of New York City: Founding Principles

On April 15, 1985, the Harvey Milk High School, an alternative school for gay and lesbian youth, opened. The school was established for several reasons:

- Young lesbian and gay students were not attending school.

- Many lesbian and gay students were at risk for dropping out of school.

- Many lesbian and gay students were chronic truants.

- "Effeminate" and "butch" young people were not being accepted in the schools.

- Youth who cross-dress were alienated in their schools.

- Many students experienced confusion about their sexuality and about coming out. They found their peers to be hostile, often to the point of violence. These young people were being verbally and physically harassed; they often voiced that they felt safer on the streets of the South Bronx than in the halls and classrooms of their high schools. This was especially true for those who were cross-dressing, those too "effeminate" or too "butch"—those who could not hide.

- Traditional schools failed to provide a safe space for lesbian and gay youth.

- Teachers were ignoring verbal harassment of gays and lesbians, but they would intervene if racial slurs were used.

- Homophobia was seen as widespread in the schools. Teachers feared being perceived as promoters of homosexuality or as being lesbian or gay.

- Gay and lexbian students were afraid to let their sexual identity become known, and this hiding process obviously takes its toll. (The hiding process includes emotional, social, and cognitive isolation, a process of deception at every level with the ability to play any role.) Students were at risk for depression and suicide.

- In 1985, 58% of Hetrick-Martin Institute youth had experienced some form of harassment (verbal, physical, or both). For these reasons and more, the Hetrick-Martin Institute, a social service agency, decided to sponsor the Harvey Milk School.

Components of the Harvey Milk School

In looking at the student population of the Harvey Milk School, 60% is male and 40% female. The student body consists predominantly of youth of color, juggling dual identities. Academically, it offers a transitional program and an alternative to traditional schools. The main goal of the school is to mainstream young people back into traditional schools and society. In fact, the records show that many have gone back to their high schools, graduated, and gone on to college and to work. The school maintains a traditional academic curriculum but also integrates historical contributions of gay men and lesbians, such as James Baldwin, Langston Hughes, Walt Whitman, Gertrude Stein, and Audre Lourde.

We know that teachers in traditional schools rarely discuss the contributions of gay and lesbian writers and historical figures. Their accomplishments need to be shared, in the same way that Black and Latino history is also integrated and infused into the curriculum, throughout the school year. This information is especially important for youth of color, to provide them with role models. Curricula should incorporate concepts of diversity on an ongoing basis.

Family response to the Harvey Milk School has been positive. For example, one mother brought her son to school after she found out about his sexual orientation from a television interview taped at the waterfront piers, where he was spending much of his time with other gay youth. When young people come to the school, parents may not know about their child's sexual orientation. However, because students need parental permission to enter the Harvey Milk High School, the process of knowing more about their child can begin.

The issue of "ghettoizing" arose when the school was founded. Despite arguments that the school might serve only to further isolate gay and lesbian youth, the Board of Education of New York City had done little to provide services in regular schools for these youth. Furthermore, the Board had done little to provide a safe place for them to get an education. Without this alternative program, these young people will ghettoize themselves to the streets. The school is proof of how many people feel it is important to get youngsters off the street, where they are at risk for drugs, prostitution, HIV infection, and other evils.

School is Another Source of Stress

Many GLB students are forced to drop out of school because of harassment regarding their sexual orientation. Combining this stressor with the problem of isolation and problems with their family, often students turn to alcohol and other drugs. In fact, in a study by the HIV Center at Columbia University, it was found that 68% of gay male youth reported alcohol use, 26% reported using alcohol once or more per week; 44% reported drug use, with 8% considering themselves to be drug dependent. Among young lesbians, 83% reported that they had used alcohol, 56% reported that they had used drugs, and 11% had used crack/cocaine in the 3 months prior to the study.

Important Facts and Suggestions

The available research indicates that

- Suicide rates among lesbian, gay and bisexual youth are high. It is estimated that up to 30% of youth suicide is committed annually by lesbian and gay youth (U.S. Department of Health and Human Services, 1989). At a parochial high school in the Bronx section of New York, there were four suicides within a 2-year period. Even though it was known that at least three of the students were having problems with their sexuality, when plans for suicide prevention were discussed, the administrators did not approve any discussion of sexuality or homosexuality with the students. By ignoring this issue, they had an ineffective prevention program.

- Lesbian, gay, and bisexual youth are an *invisible* population. Consequently, documenting violence toward them and suicide among them is difficult. Yet the data accumulated indicate the need to develop responses to their victimization.

- Bias-related violence against students in school needs to be documented, addressed, and eliminated.

- School administrators, teachers, social workers, and counselors need to be trained to confront homophobia, counsel victims of bias-related violence, and demystify homosexuality. Ongoing staff training is essential. We all have biases and we must seek to understand them. *Hate is not a family value.* The role of school social workers and counselors is to help the student and his or her family. This person has a professional obligation to refer the youth and/or the family, but not to the local homophobe. Young people are very keen in sensing even nonverbal negative messages.

- Services must be provided for those youth who need someone to talk to while going through the coming out process. The providers (social workers, counselors, doctors) must be trained and learn to be nonjudgmental. You cannot mix the teacher and counselor roles. Young people have a right to be supported, wherever they are on the continuum of sexual identity. There is the issue of privacy: the young person's right of privacy versus the parents' right to know. It cannot be predicted what parents will do when they find out their child is gay or lesbian.

- Where there are no services for lesbian, gay, and bisexual youth, it is important to develop such services. Studies by Remafedi (1994) and others demonstrate that the younger a person is at the age of "coming out," the more vulnerable he or she is and the more problems he or she will face.

- Support services for families should be provided, both in the schools and in nearby community-based organizations. There are different problems when a young person comes out to family members and when sexual orientation is disclosed.

- It is important to educate parents, as they will be the key to social change, beginning with change in the schools. Parents and Friends of Lesbians and Gays (P-FLAG) is a national organization with local chapters who are extremely effective in reaching out to other parents.

- Ultimately, all schools must provide a safe environment in which lesbian, gay, and bisexual youth can obtain an education. Challenges of adolescent development are many and diverse—sexual identity; self-esteem; friendships, including non-erotic friendships; and management of

social and sexual roles. Successful resolution necessitates that there be gay-straight alliances. Schools must provide a safe environment in which children learn tolerance and acceptance of differences. It is in the best interest of society to ensure a successful future for its young people. We must stop teaching our children to hate. Only when all youth can freely pursue their dreams, whether in a traditional high school setting, in sports, in the arts and sciences, in business schools and so on, can we as a culture claim to be fostering true humanity toward all people. In addition, young people are now growing up in the age of AIDS. If they have to leave their homes and neighborhoods to find friendships, they will become more at risk for HIV/AIDS.

- In the schools, libraries need to have age-appropriate books available on lesbian/gay themes, which de-isolate and demystify lesbian and gay lives. There need to be clubs and community centers for young people in or near the schools. *Differences need to be celebrated.*

End-of-Session Question and Answers

1. "Do you advise kids not to tell their parents?"

We do not encourage young people to tell others, because one cannot predict the responses. So often young people receive mixed messages. Young people need to develop support systems, look at the possible advantages and disadvantages of coming out, and look at the possible results. If they are prepared for negative results, such as losing one's home and family, support systems must be in place.

2. "What if a counselor or teacher has a strong feeling against homosexuality?"

It is not that person's role to make judgments. If this issue interferes with the ability of the adults to do their job in supporting the young person, then their professional behavior becomes unethical. When someone is thinking only of personal values and bias and not the concerns of the student, the young person should be referred to someone without such reservations who can help the student.

3. "In regard to HIV/AIDS prevention, what about the message to abstain?"

HIV/AIDS educators need to understand that adolescents are developing physically and emotionally and are often in the process of exploring their sexuality. Although advocating abstinence is a top priority for many counselors, we must understand that abstinence is not realistic for many youth. We need to develop educational programs that will help young people manage their sexuality safely.

Conclusion

The challenges surrounding providing students who are GLB are many and varied. In this short space, I have attempted to share information on the Harvey Milk School as a way of illustrating one approach to better serving this special population of youngsters.

References

U. S. Department of Health and Human Services. (1989). *Task force report on youth suicide.* Washington, DC: Author.

Remafedi, G. (Ed.). (1994). *Death by denial: Studies of gay and lesbian youth suicides.* Boston: Alyson.

Considerations in Working with Adolescents Who Are Gay, Lesbian, or Bisexual

Robert Rahamin
The George Washington University, Washington, DC

Philippe J. Dupont
Pathways Schools, Silver Spring, MD

Tania DuBeau
Pathways Schools, Silver Spring, MD

Chris, who was born with severe visual and hearing impairments, has led a difficult life. He has not been accepted by his peers. He came from a home that ended in divorce when he was 7 years old and his family struggled to survive financially. Chris struggled to survive in school and his community. At 15, Chris attempted suicide. He told his mother he was gay and he could not see how he could go through life with his disabilities and, worst of all, being gay. She was devastated, not because of his revelation about being gay, but because she knew the struggles he would have to face. She was desperate for any resources to help Chris.

Unfortunately, there was nowhere to turn. The service providers in the gay community were sympathetic but they were unable to address the issues of adolescents because they feared the perception that gay adults may be recruiting young people into the gay lifestyle. Social services had nothing available for gay, lesbian, or bisexual (GLB) youth. A local facility for runaway and troubled youth advised that adolescents who were GLB were at risk for being physically and emotionally abused by other residents, and they could not guarantee the safety of the individual. The school psychologist said that resources or support systems were not available within the school system. The discovery of the lack of resources was the driving force behind the establishment of "Youth Quest," a local, "grass roots" youth support group to deal with gay and lesbian issues in a safe and caring environment. Chris was the first founding member.

This is a real story that could take place in any town in the United States. It is reflective of the disparity and the lack of resources available to adolescents like Chris. It is stories like this that are symbolic of the need for professionals, schools, and communities to band together to create change on behalf of sexual minority youth.

At the Council for Children with Behavioral Disorders (CCBD) Symposium, a diverse group of individuals from New York City; Silver Spring, MD; Los Angeles, CA; and Princeton, NJ, came together. Teachers, administrators, social workers, attorneys, and university faculty, met to explore current issues confronting GLB students. Our task was to better understand the issues, to examine the best educational practices, and to highlight realistic actions for meaningful change.

Understanding the Issues Related to Providing Services to Adolescents Who Are GLB

In this chapter, the authors draw together suggestions for creating safe environments in the schools and for meeting the challenges in providing safe environments. These suggestions are linked to the accumulated remarks of the keynote speakers, literature, and observations of participants of the discussion group.

Creating Safe Environments

Every child has the right to a safe environment in which all students

- Can develop a healthy understanding of their sexual identity.
- Who are GLB can come out (self-disclosure) to peers, family, and community.
- Who are GLB are free of harassment, torment, and physical violence.
- Who have GLB parents, siblings, relatives, and friends feel acknowledged and supported.
- Can support and befriend their GLB peers without fears of being ostracized.
- Who are GLB can learn about the realities of the world outside of the "safety net" of supportive environments.
- Can learn the skills necessary to cope and self-advocate when confronted with homophobic individuals in the community outside of the "safety net."
- Can find school-sponsored support groups.

Meeting the Challenges

Critical obstacles to schools in providing safe environments include

- Insufficient number of role models in the school and community setting.
- Lack of support for teachers, administrators, and other school personnel who are GLB to come out.
- Failure of the school to address GLB-related issues in the school curriculum.
- Insufficient information about resources readily accessible to students in the libraries, on posters, or in textbooks.
- The taboo of addressing issues of sexuality in schools and communities and often in society as a whole.
- Parents' accusations that teachers who are GLB are recruiting their children into the gay lifestyle.
- The omission of "sexual orientation" from policies addressing multicultural issues and antidiscrimination.

The obstacles for students with disabilities in addition to being GLB are even greater. These students may be confronted with

- Difficulties processing information because of their learning difficulties.
- The stigma of having a disability in GLB support groups.
- Social imperception: challenges of reading the social cues in the environment which highlight safety (a safe place vs. an unsafe place).

- Being at greater risk of being sexually or physically victimized.

Parallels have often been made about the issues challenging ethnic groups and GLB groups. The similarities between the two groups include

- The need to develop the coping skills to deal with a stigmatized role.
- The importance of developing a support network, including role models.

The differences between the two groups include

- The ability for ethnic groups to readily identify others who are of the same group, but adolescents who are GLB are not able to do so.
- The ability for ethnic groups to seek support from their family members and often their community, but adolescents who are GLB are not readily able to do so.

Because of the lack of role models and resources, adolescents who are GLB are not able to see themselves reflected in their environment at a time when their identity development is crucial. This contributes to

- Fears of coming out.
- Feelings of shame, depression, and isolation.
- A low sense of self-worth and self-esteem.
- A high rate of drug and alcohol addiction.
- A disproportionately high rate of suicide and suicidal attempts.

Examining Best Educational Practices: Incorporating the Needs of Adolescents Who Are GLB Within School Goals

It does not appear to be the size of the city that determines the availability of services for students who are GLB. Data indicate that neither the public nor the private sector is more supportive of the concerns of students who are GLB or who are struggling with their sexual identities. Rather, it is attitudes, beliefs, and fears of a community that determine the willingness and courage to begin to confront the controversial issues related to providing services to adolescents who are GLB. In some places, services have grown out of the experience of one person touched by the life of a GLB teen, such as in Chris's town. In other places, services have grown out of the efforts of a group of people identifying the need of adolescents who are GLB and appealing to the emotions of the board of education, the parent-teacher-student associations, or the county officials.

Potential Services

A continuum of services and activities is needed at both the community and school levels.

Potential services identified within communities include

- Support groups within the gay community, such as Gay, Lesbian, Straight Teachers Network (GLSTN).
- Mental health service agencies open to addressing the needs of individuals who are GLB or who are struggling with their sexual identities.

Potential services and activities that may assist schools include

- Development of extracurricular support groups for students (i.e., Gay/Straight Student Association).
- Use of school newspapers to provide GLB support group information.
- Requirement of staff development training for educators about the needs of students who are GLB.
- A curriculum that acknowledges or highlights GLB issues in subject areas including history, literature, and arts (multicultural approach to education).
- Implementation of policies that reflect protection for the rights of all students (antidiscrimination policies).

Highlighting Realistic Actions That Could Result in a More Accepting School Climate

We live in busy times and not everyone can dedicate additional time and energy to the cause; however, it is important to recognize that people can commit to making a change. This process must begin with individuals, school systems, and communities.

The process of creating change focuses on

- Creating awareness.
- Adjusting and broadening beliefs and attitudes.
- Building skills and increasing personal knowledge.
- Promoting advocacy for all students.

Creating Awareness

It is important that people develop an awareness of

- Their own sexuality.
- The needs of adolescents who are GLB or who are struggling with their sexual identities.
- Their power and ability to make a difference.

Adjusting and Broadening Beliefs and Attitudes

It is beliefs and attitudes that are at the heart of the controversy surrounding homosexuality and bisexuality. Before attitudes can be reshaped, people need to be able to honestly identify their beliefs and attitudes, including

- Discomfort with issues of sexuality and, specifically, sex.
- Fears of homosexuals.
- Feelings that homosexuality is a sin.
- Concerns about the origins of homosexuality (genetic, hormonal, or psychological).
- Belief that homosexuality is a choice.
- Tolerance of individuals who are GLB, if they do not talk about it.

Building Skills and Increasing Personal Knowledge

It is only after beliefs and attitudes have been identified that one can begin to confront personal fears, discomfort, and intolerance and educate people about the realities of the experience of being GLB. One can begin to teach the skills to develop tolerance, understanding, and respect for *all* students and *all* people. The process of changing attitudes and beliefs is a significant challenge. It cannot always be accomplished in one staff development program, one class, one semester-long course, or sometimes even in a lifetime. However, the efforts need to be made to change the attitudes of one person at a time.

Promoting Advocacy for All Students

The resulting combined efforts of those who have always been supportive and those who become supportive of adolescents who are GLB can make phenomenal changes through their advocacy for the rights of all students. It is everybody's responsibility to change educational practices and community responses. The responsibility to survive in intolerant schools and communities should not fall on the adolescent who is GLB.

The advocacy for the rights of students who are GLB becomes the individual and collective responsibility of people at all levels including

- Administrators.
- Parent groups.
- Parents.
- Teachers.
- Lawyers.
- University personnel.
- High school students.
- College students.
- Boards of education.

- Local, state, and federal politicians.
- Churches.
- Media.

Bringing about change through the collaborative efforts of these groups promises to be a challenging process, which highlights the need for all people to support each other along the way. Every day there is an opportunity to make someone aware of the issues of individuals who are GLB and the challenges they face.

There are variety of ways for individuals to get involved:

- GLB adults can mentor adolescents who are GLB.
- Volunteer on a hotline for adolescents.
- Volunteer to sponsor a support group for gay/straight adolescents.
- Write informational articles for local publications and professional journals.
- Write informational articles for magazines, and newspapers.
- Write editorials in response to articles related to GLB issues.
- Conduct research with adolescents who are GLB.
- Gain the support of existing groups, such as Parent/Teacher/Student Associations (PTSA).
- Provide sensitivity training to all students and school personnel.
- Train police departments.
- Encourage the support of "straight" (heterosexual) people.
- Develop a GLB task force within existing professional organizations.
- Present workshops at conferences.

- Encourage your religious institution to become a welcoming congregation (open to GLB members).
- Identify yourself to your friends, relatives, and coworkers as being supportive of the rights for individuals who are GLB.

Resources

There are a growing number of resources for adolescents who are GLB or who are struggling with their sexual identities and for adults who are striving to be of assistance. The reader is referred to a list of valuable resources included at the conclusion of the volume.

Conclusion

Until a plan is in place, the struggle will continue for students like Chris. How can meaningful change begin to occur so that adolescents who are GLB do not continue to isolate themselves, drop out of school, and contemplate suicide? Dewey (1916) spoke of a progressive society recognizing the preciousness of individuality and allowing for intellectual freedom, the gifts of diversity, and interests in its educational practices. This highlights the importance of inclusiveness and creating environments and curricula to meet the needs of all students. Change must begin with individuals, school systems, and communities if schools are to be better places for all children and youth.

Reference

Dewey, J. (1916). *Democracy and education: An introduction to the philosophy of education*. New York: Macmillan.

Safe Supportive Schools for All Youth:
A Call to Action

Ann Fitzsimons-Lovett
Doctoral Candidate, Special Education
University of North Texas, Denton, Texas

Mary Gale Budzisz
Teacher of Adolescents
Milwaukee Public Schools, Milwaukee, Wisconsin

This chapter reflects the thoughts of seven professionals representing public and private education, universities, and health and social service agencies comprising one of several discussions groups. The discussions centered on three major themes: (a) identifying the needs of adolescents who are gay, lesbian, or bisexual (GLB) and ways to meet these needs within the school setting; (b) obstacles to meeting identified needs; and (c) recommendations to overcome these obstacles and successfully meeting the needs of these youth.

Meeting the Needs of AdolescentsWho Are GLB Within School Settings

Adolescents who are GLB face the arduous task of coping simultaneously with the demands of two challenging processes: growing up and coming out (Hunter, 1996). At a time when being like peers and fitting in with the crowd is of paramount importance, this group may begin to fully realize just how different they are. The realization that they have affectional orientations that differ from their heterosexual peers and that this orientation goes against societally accepted norms places incredible stress on sexual minority adolescents. While a large percentage of youth who are GLB manage this stress in a productive way and do not let it interfere with their educational or vocational goals, many do not.

A significant number of adolescents who are GLB respond to the stress of being "different" by isolating themselves physically and socially (Hunter & Schaecher, 1995; Martin & Hetrick, 1988). This fact is evidenced when one considers the higher-than-average number of adolescents with "different" sexual orientations who abuse alcohol and other drugs, attempt suicide, drop out of school, or fail academic courses (Rotheram-Borus, et al., 1994).

This discussion group agreed that the overarching goal for schools should be to create places where adolescents who are GLB feel accepted and valued as contributing members of the microsystem. Further, we concluded that schools must provide environments that are safe and supportive for all students.

Ensuring a Safe School Environment

The provision of an environment that is safe and non-threatening for all students must be a minimum standard for all schools. Yet research indicates that this minimal expectation is not being met in our nation's schools. Accounts of verbal and physical violence and harassment of students who are perceived as being GLB are commonplace (Berrill, 1990). The hostile environment in schools encountered daily by these youth results in students having to spend an inordinate amount of time and energy trying to keep the "secret" of their affectional orientation hidden. Ultimately, the situation results in the students having less energy to focus on academic and extracurricular pursuits, which in turn leads to academic failure and isolation within the school setting (Hunter & Schaecher, 1995; Mallon, 1996).

Before schools can begin to address the many needs of adolescents who are GLB, they need to adopt policies that send a loud, strong message to school personnel and to the public at large that violence and harassment against any individual or group, including students who are GLB, will not be tolerated under any circumstances. Clear consequences must be established to address violations of this policy. Schools can make changes relatively easily by expanding their existing policies and students' code of conduct handbooks to include sexual orientation under their discrimination policies. These changes need to be clarified to the school constituency through meetings and communications. Schools can learn from the way "sexual harassment" policies were introduced in the early 1990s.

Once policies are in place to make certain that the school is a safe place for all youth, it is vital that action plans be established to ensure the consistent adherence to and implementation of these policies. Action plans will guarantee that policies make the essential transition from rhetoric to practice. Violations of policy need to be carefully monitored and reported to the proper authorities. Given the sensitive nature of these types of incidents, schools may wish to consider establishing a hotline number where students—both victims and onlookers—can call to report incidents without fear of repercussion. Schools need to set up procedures to deal with violators of the policies. For example, students who engage in verbal abuse of their peers who are GLB might be required to participate in corrective instructional discipline procedures, such as attending a minicourse on diversity.

Providing a Supportive Atmosphere

While upholding and enforcing the right of adolescents who are GLB to have a safe school environment is a necessary first step, it alone is not sufficient. In addition to addressing safety issues, schools need to decide how they will provide appropriate support for individuals who are GLB. Traditionally, when school personnel have felt that they are not equipped to meet the needs of a particular student, the course of action has been to refer the student to special education services or to an outside agency for help. This is not, however, an effective approach in meeting the needs of adolescents who are GLB. Other than in a few exceptional cases, social service agencies have been equally negligent in their ability to serve the needs of this group of adolescents. Often these social service agencies (e.g., mental health agencies, child welfare establishments, juvenile justice authorities) have adopted the same stance as schools with regard to this issue; that is, they have behaved as if there were no adolescents who are GLB and have therefore failed to address this issue. Evidence of this can be seen in their lack of service provisions for this group and in their negligence in providing appropriate preservice or continuing education to address issues related to this population.

A primary step in providing support to students who are GLB is the acknowledgment of their existence. Schools can engage in a variety of activities that demonstrate their recognition and support of these students:

- Sponsor gay-straight alliance support groups.
- Post advertisements pertaining to GLB youth clubs or other services in conspicuous places.
- Ensure easy access to an adequate supply of library books that provide accurate, current information on GLB issues.
- Acknowledge Gay Pride History month in June.
- Display the pink triangle or diversity flag in key locations around campus to denote a safe environment. Faculty may display the symbols to let students know they are supportive.

If adolescents who are GLB are to receive adequate support in the school, then it is essential that all school personnel are empowered to meet their needs. A primary route to empowerment is appropriate staff preparation. Training needs to be delivered at both the preservice and inservice levels that provides accurate, relevant, and current information on human sexuality issues. A central element in this training will be to have staff members examine and confront their own religious and cultural feelings about homosexuality. Until staff members have internalized an attitude of respect for differences in youth, they cannot effectively transmit this respect to their students. This group recognized that changing deep-rooted perceptions by school personnel is a long, slow process; however it can be done.

Identifying a single person or group of people who become the resident "gay experts" in the school is to be avoided because this allows all other school personnel to abdicate their responsibility to become informed about this topic.

The homophobic attitudes of many youth in our nation's schools must be addressed if adolescents who are GLB are ever to feel truly supported within the school environment. Homophobia hurts everyone, not just GLB youth and their families. It hurts everyone because it perpetuates ignorance and intolerance for individual differences (Hunter & Schaecher, 1995). Homophobia should be addressed on two levels, both directly and indirectly. The policy changes suggested earlier and the activities that schools can engage in are key *direct* strategies that schools can use to announce to the public that they are aware that this particular group of students exist and that they are supportive of all students.

Schools can, as a matter of routine, *indirectly* confront homophobic attitudes by acknowledging the contributions in almost every school subject (e.g., math, literature, arts, music) of famous individuals who are (were) GLB. Extending or expanding upon current course offerings in health, sexuality, or life skills to focus on GLB issues and acceptance and tolerance of all kinds of diversity is another strategy suggested to combat homophobic attitudes in schools.

The phrase "he/she is gay," is one that is being used often by students when they wish to say something negative about an individual. One of the group participants mentioned that she handles this daily occurrence in her classroom by saying "Gay is okay." Giving students simple messages like this on a consistent basis can prompt heterosexual students to examine their use of words such as *fag* or *gay*. It can also communicate to students who are GLB that this is a place where they are accepted and where prejudicial comments about their lifestyle will not be entertained.

In our efforts to create safe and supportive school environments for adolescents who are GLB, schools should also acknowledge the existence of gay and lesbian parents. Increasing numbers of children in schools are living with parents who are gay or lesbian. Often these parents are reluctant to discuss their personal situation with school personnel because they fear that their child-rearing capabilities will be viewed with suspicion. Schools need to be sensitive to the needs of these parents and the needs of children who come from households where there are "two fathers" or "two mothers." A simple minimal measure that schools need to take is to ensure that all communications sent home for parental review use inclusive language and do not assume that every child is living with heterosexual parents (e.g., address communications "Dear Parents/Caregivers").

Obstacles to Meeting the Needs of Youth Who Are GLB in Schools

Three main obstacles to implementing changes in schools that would create safe and supportive environments for "all" youth are fear, a laissez-faire attitude, and a "here we go again" attitude.

Fear

Fear comes from many sources. Parents are afraid of what topics might be discussed under the label of "human sexuality." Teachers and administrators are slow to champion the cause of provision of services for GLB youth because they fear repercussion from increasingly conservative school boards. Many teach-

ers, staff, and parents argue that permitting actions such as the establishment of Gay--Straight Alliance Support Groups is tantamount to recruiting adolescents into a GLB lifestyle.

Laissez-Faire Attitude

The laissez-faire attitude is reflected in the refusal of schools and other service agencies to acknowledge the existence of adolescents who are GLB. Further, these institutions refuse to acknowledge that many adolescents who are *not* gay, lesbian, or bisexual come from households where the *parents* are gay or lesbian. If this laissez-faire attitude is allowed to prevail, then the continuation of enforced invisibility for this group of students (and their parents) will be promoted. If, on the other hand, schools acknowledge the existence of youth who are GLB, then schools will have to do something to address their needs. Adopting a laissez-faire approach may be viewed as the path of least resistance.

"Here We Go Again" Attitude

A final obstacle to meeting the needs in the schools of adolescents who are GLB is the "here we go again" attitude held by many parents, teachers, and the public at large. This attitude reflects the viewpoint that adolescents who are GLB are just another disenfranchised group who want their recognition. There is considerable concern that schools are already overburdened with mandates (and/or public expectation) to address societal issues including violence, racism, teenage pregnancy, and substance abuse. Addressing bias and discrimination based on sexual orientation often is viewed as "just another burden" and that too much time already is being spent on addressing societal issues in school rather than providing academic instruction. We must take steps to change this situation.

Recommendations for Overcoming Identified Obstacles

Two key strategies were identified by the group to assist in overcoming the identified obstacles: communication and incremental change. The root fear is a lack of knowledge and the adherence to myths when discussing issues related to affectional orientation. Clear communication can help alleviate some of the fears of parents, school staff, and school boards. All stakeholders need to be fully informed of the breadth of any policy changes or proposed activities. The provision of clear, accurate information when training personnel and working with the student body at large needs to be a priority. In order to prevent sensationalistic or biased news reporting in the media, it is especially important that regular communication be established with the local media when new school policies or activities are introduced. Establishing open communication channels with the local media can also help to ensure that the general public receives an accurate report of the rationale and need for the new policies and activities.

Using small incremental steps to initiate the policy changes and introduce suggested activities was a key recommendation made by the group. We agreed that pushing these issues into people's faces would inhibit, rather than assist, schools in meeting the needs of adolescents who are GLB. A soft-pedaling technique would definitely appear to be in order. We agreed that the most palatable way to approach the issue and to gain support is to weave it into the whole "diversity" tapestry.

To overcome the attitudinal obstacle that schools have "too much on their plate already" without having to address the issue of adolescents who are GLB, schools need to stress that none of the proposed actions constitute entirely new programs. They are merely suggestions for expanding current policies and programs to ensure that they are inclusive of all students. In fact, we strongly suggest that a discrete curriculum related to GLB issues does not need to be developed. These issues need to be infused into the regular curriculum as a routine part of the daily school experience.

Conclusion

Schools and social service agencies have a responsibility to serve and provide comprehensive, culturally appropriate services for all youth. For too long, adolescents who are GLB have not been included. Limited substantive efforts have been made to address the specific needs of this group. Immediate changes in policy, service provisions, and personnel training need to occur to ensure that schools do not continue to ignore the specific and urgent needs of approximately one out of every ten of America's youth.

References

Berrill, K. (1990). Anti-gay violence and victimization in the United States. *Journal of Interpersonal Violence, 5*(3), 274-294.

Hunter, J. (1996, February). *The challenge toward a more inclusive tomorrow: Knowledge, commitment and action.* Paper presented at the Council for Children with Behavioral Disorders Symposium on Understanding Individual Differences: What Educators Should Know About Adolescents Who are Gay, Lesbian, or Bisexual. New York City, NY.

Hunter, J., & Schaecher, R. (1995). Gay and lesbian adolescents. In R. L. Edwards & J. G. Hopps (Eds.), *Encyclopedia of social work*. Washington, DC: National Association of Social Workers.

Mallon, G. (1996, February). *Schools and communities who have embraced the challenge: Best educational practices.* Paper presented at the Council for Children with Behavioral Disorders Symposium on Understanding Individual Differences: What Educators Should Know About Adolescents Who are Gay, Lesbian, or Bisexual. New York City, NY.

Martin, D., & Hetrick, D. (1988). The stigmatization of the gay and lesbian adolescents. *Journal of Homosexuality, 15*(1-2), 163-183.

Rotheram-Borus, M., Rosario, M., Mayer-Bahlburg, H., Koopman, C., Dopkins, S., & Davies, M. (1994). Sexual and substance abuse acts of gay and bisexual male adolescents in New York City. *Journal of Sex Research, 31*(1), 47-57.

Adolescents Who Are Gay, Lesbian, or Bisexual: The Schools' Challenge

Nomsa Gwalla-Ogisi
University of Wisconsin-Whitewater

Shelly Sikorski
University of Wisconsin-Whitewater

The road to adolescence is paved with numerous opportunities and challenges. In a society that assumes heterosexuality is the "norm," youth who are gay, lesbian, or bisexual (GLB) experience significant difficulties in our schools and communities. For youth who are GLB, adolescence offers challenges and conflicts that stem from their sexual orientation. While some youth who are GLB are able to cope with the stress related to their sexual identity, many are unable to do so (Hunter & Schaecher, 1987; 1995). Because youth spend a significant portion of their lives in school, these stressors are often exacerbated by the way schools respond and react. The following reflects the discussion and recommendations that emerged from one group of the participants who attended the CCBD symposium.

Understanding the Issues Related to Providing Services to Adolescents Who Are GLB

Heterosexual adolescents face stressors related to adolescence often because they are not fully informed about the physical, psychological, and social changes taking place in their bodies and lives. Adolescents who are GLB experience even greater distress because of their emerging or newly found identities. Hunter and Schaecher (1987; 1995), Pawlowski (1996), and others assert that most young people who are GLB become aware of their difference in sexual orientation during adolescence. The distress experienced by youth who are GLB is increased because of the conscious and deliberate exclusion of information about physical, psychological, and social changes critical for self-awareness and self-understanding. Additionally, youth who are GLB who are rejected by parents do not have the benefit of parental guidance. For youth unable to cope with having a different sexual orientation, many problems arise (e.g., confusion, conflict, preoccupation with hiding the GLB identity, self-depreciation or even self-hate, isolation, low or poor self-esteem, fear of being discovered, guilt, distrust, relationship problems, depression, and many others; Hunter & Schaecher, 1995).

The youth who are able to cope with the new identity and who then "come out" (i.e., publicly disclose their sexual orientation), deal with a different set of challenges (e.g., discrimination, rejection, isolation, physical violence, verbal abuse, condemnation, constraints in career options, hate, and legal problems). It is no wonder that some of the youth who are GLB, given the enormity of these daily life stressors, turn to alcohol to numb the pain; others choose suicide to escape the pain.

Challenges Faced by the Schools in Finding, Understanding, and Recognizing Adolescents Who Are GLB

Our society has a history of viewing differences in people in a simplistic manner: either good or bad; superior or inferior. Being GLB within this society often is perceived as bad, wrong, or deviant. Institutionalized rejection of individuals who are GLB is evident in many schools and other social systems (Durby, 1994). The school climate frequently is either hostile or silent, thus rendering students who are GLB afraid or invisible. Faced with life in such environments, these youth do not feel safe to disclose who they are, much less communicate what they need from schools.

Another barrier to finding and understanding GLB youth in schools is fear. Heterosexual youth and teachers, and youth and teachers who may be questioning their sexual orientations, often distance themselves from youth who are "out." (They fear being perceived as GLB and thus suffer the same negative treatment to which GLB youth are subjected.) Youth who are GLB also "hide" because they fear violence against them.

Schools located in highly homophobic communities tend not to identify youth who are GLB, fearing negative public opinion and consequences that could affect school personnel, public support, and funding. Several members of the group represented in this chapter reported personal experiences of youth who are GLB who were intimidated or were attacked both at school and in the community. Some experienced early exposure to the police because of their fights to defend their dignity and their lives.

This group felt that it is critical for schools to involve families of youth who are GLB. Beliefs about these youth and their families' stages of coping may influence their involvement with schools. Parents of GLB youth represented within the dialogue group reported that they experienced the same fears and stressors about coming out to acknowledge and accept youth who are GLB as the youth did in accepting themselves.

Our view is that an understanding of the coming-out process could assist schools in determining ways to support and reach youth who are GLB. It is generally believed there are four stages of coming-out experienced by both the GLB youth and their parents: denial, confrontation, exploration of what it means to be GLB or a parent of a youth who is GLB, and, finally, acceptance.

How Are the Challenges Similar to or Different From Those Faced by Schools in Dealing With Diversity Within the Student Body?

Schooling is a dynamic process in which competing interests, values, and ways of being are at work every day in complex and contradictory ways. Today, schools more than ever before, are experiencing a sense of urgency about not only understanding the diversity of learners but also being responsive to this diversity.

Out of our discussion, we agreed on several ways in which the experiences of youth who are GLB are similar to and different from the experiences of racial minorities or peers with exceptionalities. The following paragraphs summarize our discussion.

Oppression/Discrimination

In today's schools, youth who are GLB, youth of color, and youth with special needs often experience some oppression and discrimination that takes many forms: (a) silenced, shamed—public and private pain of being forced to be ashamed of sexual orientation or skin color or disability; (b) decreased expectations—marginalization; (c) invisibility—no images representative of their experience; (d) lack of role models; (e) rejection; alienation—being excluded, isolated, socially ostracized; and (f) perception of incompetence—presumed racial inferiority—presumed evilness of being GLB. An inability to cope with the challenges posed by the system is seen as evidence of incompetence rather than an intolerant environment. Insensitive teaching approaches disempower GLB youth, youth of color, and those with special needs.

Identity

Youth who are GLB, like youth of color and those with disabilities are treated as though they do not have individual identities. Behaviors of individuals who are GLB often are stereotypically generalized for the entire GLB community. Individual identities are subsumed by group stereotypes. The difference here is that youth of color never can hide their skin color, race, and culture, but youth who are GLB could choose to hide their sexual identity for the sake of "acceptance." This acceptance, which is based on lies, creates other stressors for the youth—stressors stemming from being "found out" (i.e., sexual orientation discovered by others).

Examining Best Practices: Incorporating the Needs of Adolescents Within School Goals

There was agreement in this dialogue group that many schools are not responsive to the needs of youth who are GLB. In order for these youth to thrive in schools and communities, schools have to transform their practices. For schools to be responsive, they have to meet basic needs that have been identified as central to the resiliency of sexual minority youth (Brendtro, Brokenleg, & Van Bakern, 1990; Joseph, 1994).

Schools in which youth who are GLB succeed are schools that are inclusive (Durby, 1994; Kennedy, 1994; Niento, 1992). Such schools are said to be *diversity competent*. Being diversity competent means that school personnel understand the development, behaviors, world view, and cultural experiences of learners and the way these experiences influence how youth learn and view themselves and the world. Such schools strive to become better informed about the diversity of their student body. These schools tend to be safe havens for GLB staff to come-out so that they can serve as role models for youth who are GLB or who are struggling with their sexual identities. Schools that nurture academic success for youth who are GLB create a climate within which all students feel psychologically and physically safe that generates excitement about learning, one that defines ways of being in relationships as a group, that finds the different ways in which youth are smart (their multiple intelligences [Kennedy, 1994]), and that uses relevant and research-based instruction.

Exemplary schools construct curricula that include GLB concerns (e.g., in health and sexuality education). Instead of focusing only on the perception of two genders—male and female—schools could incorporate research and findings on the ways of viewing gender: (a) external gender—outside body genitals; (b) internal gender—inside body (e.g., fallopian tubes, testicles); (c) chromosomal gender XY or XX: masculinized female, feminized male, and blended gender with outside genitals different from inside gender (male outside with female internal organs); (d) assigned gender—chosen by parents to be performed medically on a child with both male and female organs (often selecting the gender with the most dominant organs); (e) gender of identity—in which the brain of the growing fetus selects a gender (e.g., male fetus later develops into a female [Pawlowski, 1996]).

Highlighting Realistic Action That Could Result in More Accepting School Climates

It can be argued that an accepting school climate is one that meets youth's basic need for belonging, competence/mastery, independence, interdependence, and altruism (Brendtro et al., 1990). The first basic need is that of belonging. Belonging, being connected, implies a sense of strong ties, bonding with family and the larger community, and a sharing of acceptance and mutual concern critical for empowerment.

Actions to Support Youth and Create a Climate of Belonging

- Communicate and encourage students to recognize that they are co-owners of the school and classroom. The language used by adults should reflect this (e.g., "our school," "our classroom," instead of the principal's or teacher's school or classroom).

- Youth who are GLB should see evidence of the school's respect and value for diversity and the contributions of the diverse groups. The physical

school environment should have significant images representative of all the diverse groups (e.g., posters of prominent individuals who are [were] GLB). This action sends a message to young people that they are not invisible, they are not marginalized, excluded, or disempowered.

- Plan and provide experiences that allow youth to work on peer group cohesiveness, staff/youth bonding, community connections. Examples include community adult mentors; cross-age linkages where youth work with and mentor younger children; administration/staff/student cohesion and mutual support. Provide systems of communication that are open and which guarantee emotional and physical safety by outlawing cruelty, put-downs, and ostracization. Develop harassment policies accepted by school boards.

- Create a safe environment, including job security, for teachers to come-out so that GLB youth can have role models and people to talk to who share their experiences.

One group member described an activity that has been of significant support to GLB youth in a Cincinnati school. The school plans a "Homecoming Celebration" during which former graduates of the school, who are GLB, are invited from all over the country to visit the school, share their experiences and successes, and support youth as long-distance mentors. These adults serve as role models.

Three other members of the group, who work at the same school in New York, shared what their school does to create belonging. They highlighted coalitions between GLB and heterosexual youth. Young people formed a "Tolerance Club," open to all students. It coordinates activities that address diversity issues and serves as a platform for dialogue and exchanges for the school. All members felt such a club should have a staff member as an advisor or perhaps a staff member and a community volunteer. Youth need adults to talk to who are able to articulate their needs to the system. The club serves as a catalyst for change and for tackling sensitive topics.

In Whitewater, Wisconsin, students helped to address issues of homophobia, racism, and sexism by planning and presenting activities that helped the participants experience through role plays, simulations, and dramatizations what it feels like to be oppressed, discriminated against, or alienated as a result of differences. The students developed a "Tunnel of Oppression" experience that the participants "live through" for an hour and a half. Afterwards they discuss actions necessary in order to create environments of belonging. We believe that this strategy can be adapted for any setting at the middle and high school levels.

Students at the University of Wisconsin-Whitewater helped develop a process they used as consultants with several school groups and classes to facilitate attitudinal and behavioral change. The process involves the following steps: (a) plan for awareness; (b) plan for self-reflection; (c) plan for change; (d) guide the process of setting goals; (e) plan for a support network; (f) plan for opportunities; and (g) plan for celebration of change.

Actions to Create an Environment Where Youth Can be Competent and Feel Able to Achieve

When youth who are GLB are in a state of constant fear, discouragement, marginalization, and alienation, they soon lose their motivation for learning and give up taking any risk to learn. Their creative potential is never realized. This dialogue group suggested several activities to respond to the challenges faced by the schools. Faculty and staff should be trained not to assume heterosexuality, to understand the needs of diverse learners, and to equip them with skills to meet those needs. Teacher preparation institutions should play a significant role in preparing future teachers to

- Examine their assumptions about youth who are GLB and other diversity issues.

- Examine their beliefs, experiences, and biases.

- Learn language and communication patterns that are sensitive to GLB youth.

- Set high expectations for all youth.

- Use responsive instructional practices.

- Learn to develop curriculum that is inclusive of diversity, acknowledging GLB issues.

- Become acquainted with GLB literature that should be integrated into the curriculum.

Schools should incorporate experiences for youth that foster resiliency. The group perceived resiliency as "the capacity to survive, to progress through difficulty, to bounce back, to move on positively—again and again in life" (Joseph, 1994). To become resilient, youth should be exposed to information to enhance self-knowledge, understanding of others, decision making, teaming, collaboration, cooperation and conflict-management skills. Classroom teaching could use *Learning Buddies* and *Student Learning Teams*. *Learning Buddies* is a system used to help students connect with other peers and to enhance learning skills (e.g., students in a classroom are paired and given "bonding time;" then each pair selects ways in which they will help each other, such as taking notes for an absent partner, affirming and following up with

the partner on assignments, problem solving, studying together).

Student Learning Teams, on the other hand, are triads or quads that are formed weekly to do a variety of things, such as comparing notes after a presentation, dialoguing about concerns, quizzing each other, and providing feedback to each other.

Actions to Meet Youth's Basic Need for Independence

Autonomy, responsibility for one's actions, and responsible action toward others can be facilitated by schools through several activities:

- Involve youth in the decision-making process in school activities. Allow youth, with adult guidance, to plan some of the school activities. Empower youth with self-governance in significant areas that affect them (e.g., input into harassment policies, discipline policies).

- Develop a resource list for youth, consisting of local community groups as well as national GLB support and information groups. Expose youth to leadership experiences. Above all, teach youth *how* to learn, not just *what* to learn—this way they can truly be independent thinkers.

- Provide youth with opportunities to learn about and find healthy ways of having "fun." Empower them with skills to resist negative peer pressure and to become assertive, disciplined, and confident youth. Plan "activity nights" on Fridays that keep youth off the streets and in safe environments monitored by adults. For example, a youth group in Milwaukee, under the leadership of Anthony Long and Timothy Rogers, learned videotaping and editing skills. The youth started what became a live call-in TV show called "Troubled Teens" that could discuss GLB-related topics and other adolescent issues. Such programs empower the voices of youth and their issues.

Actions to Meet the Need for Generosity and Interdependence

Generosity and altruism communicate caring, empathy, recognition of our interdependence. The dialogue group suggested two actions that could promote school climates within which youth experience altruism and interdependence:

- Develop mentoring programs where youth are mentored by GLB adults.

- Encourage community service. To tear down community barriers, youth can contribute time to GLB and non-GLB organizations in the community and plan community education and fun projects.

Conclusion

In this chapter, we have sought to capture the main ideas presented by one dialogue group at the CCBD Symposium. The challenges that youth face in school as well as the challenges that schools face in identifying and meeting the needs of learners who are GLB are formidable.

As a group, we felt the urgency to prevent the alienation, fear, violence, and despair that is experienced by these youth in today's schools. Transforming schools involves much more than eliminating unfavorable references to GLB. It also involves making substantive changes in how schools view diversity, and it requires the development of curriculum and teaching practices that are responsive to diversity.

References

Brendtro, L., Brokenleg, M., & Van Bakern, S. (1990). *Reclaiming youth at risk: Our hope for the future.* Bloomington, IN: National Educational Service.

Durby, D. (1994). Gay, lesbian and bisexual youth. *Journal of Gay and Lesbian Social Services 34*(1), 1-37.

Hunter, J., & Schaecher, R. (1987). *Stresses on lesbian and gay adolescents in schools.* Washington, DC: National Association of Social Workers.

Hunter, J., & Schaecher, R. (1995). *Gay and lesbian adolescents.* Washington, DC: Encyclopedia of Social Work.

Joseph, J. M. (1994). *The resilient child: Preparing today's youth for tomorrow's world.* New York: Plenum Press.

Kennedy, M. (1994, January). Finding the smart in every child. *Good Housekeeping,* 50-53.

Niento, S. (1992). *Affirming diversity.* New York: Longman.

Pawlowski, W. (1996, February). *Keynote Address.* Symposium conducted by CCBD on "Understanding Individual Differences, What Educators Should Know about Gay, Lesbian, and Bisexual Youth." Teacher's College, Columbia University, New York.

CREATING EDUCATIONAL ENVIRONMENTS THAT VALUE GAY AND LESBIAN YOUTH: A SYNOPSIS OF A PANEL PRESENTATION

TOM MCINTYRE
HUNTER COLLEGE, NEW YORK CITY

JOEL VON ORNSTEINER
NEW YORK CITY SCHOOLS

The concluding session of the symposium featured a panel discussion on issues facing teachers and students who are gay or lesbian. Panel members recruited from New York City educational facilities were Jonathan Berger, student and co-head of the Gay/Straight Alliance at Fieldston High School; Jason Fleetwood-Boldt, student at Calhoun High School; Talia Young, student and co-head of the Gay/Straight Alliance at Breary High School; Donna Checkan, teacher of physical education at the Spence School and co-head of the New York Metro Area Gay, Lesbian and Straight Teacher Network (GLSTN); Matthew Stewart, teacher of the performing arts at the Spence School, and co-head of New York Metro GLSTN, and Joel Von Ornsteiner, former special education teacher who is now a school psychologist for the New York City School System. Tom McIntyre, Professor of Special Education at Hunter College of the City University of New York served as the panel moderator.

The Panel Presentation

Questions and answers are paraphrased but represent the content of the discussion. (Questions were asked by the moderator unless otherwise indicated.)

Q: (To the students) Today, the discussion up to this point has involved adults talking about students. Because you are actively involved in developing supportive school atmospheres for youth who are gay, lesbian, or bisexual (GLB), what do you perceive to be the major concerns, issues, and challenges for these teens in today's schools?

A: First and foremost is the impact of homophobic attitudes and beliefs from many straight students and teachers. We are working hard to educate them so that the apathy or abuse that sometimes surfaces is transformed into interest and acceptance.

Q: (To the students) You are all leaders in Gay/Straight Alliances at different high schools. What is the purpose of the Alliances? What activities do they undertake? What occurs at your meetings? How do you gain the support and enrollment of straight students, teens who are unsure of their sexual orientation, and GLB students who are concerned about negative consequences if their orientation becomes known to others?

A: Our primary goal is to reduce homophobia in our schools. We present workshops and engage in other educational and awareness activities. In addition to planning and implementing events, during meetings we discuss incidents in our schools and articles, books, movies, television shows, and recent events affecting the GLB community. We welcome everyone into our groups, although it is sometimes difficult to recruit both homosexual and heterosexual students because of the ridicule and rejection they might face from others. We are making progress in gaining acceptance, but we still have much to achieve.

Q: (To the entire panel) The professionals in the audience today are interested in creating educational environments that welcome and value youth who are GLB. How can professionals go about doing that, especially in schools and districts where that need is not recognized or resistance to these efforts is present? How do they gain the support of *school boards, superintendents, building administrators, teachers, parents, and the community at large when attempting to create safe and supportive school environments for the GLB population?*

A: The most important step is the first one—finding and creating support among members of the school community for proposed programs and undertakings. It is important to obtain both internal (school-based) and external (community) support. This is done by making personal contacts and engaging in educational efforts to help the individuals involved in decision making move along the continuum from awareness to tolerance to acceptance. Depending on the proposed services and the nature of the community, several approaches might be used to garner support, such as personal communication, presentations and workshops, media coverage, community involvement, and so forth. Many key players become more receptive to the proposed endeavors once they are assured that the suggested programs are not meant to "create" homosexual youth or promote "the homosexual lifestyle."

It is important to make clear that the proposed programs and support systems are designed to try to guarantee that the learning environment provides physical and psychological safety to youngsters who are often denied this protection. At times, this means reminding educators of their obligation to meet the personal and educational needs of *all* students. It is also important to convince influential and pivotal individuals who are already supportive to join in efforts to influence others. Assurances from those on the "inside" help to gain the support of others.

To summarize; it is important to develop a general positive consensus among the important players before program implementation. When supportive administrators force requirements on an unwilling staff and community, there is a good chance that the program will be sabotaged, resulting in conflict rather than cooperation. Raising nonacceptance to tolerance, and later to the higher levels of acceptance and celebration requires an ongoing educational effort.

Q: (To the teachers) Your organization, the Gay/Lesbian/ Straight Teacher Network, known as GLSTN, is a national organization that provides support to teachers who are gay and lesbian. What are the main concerns of those you serve? What services does your organization provide to these educators?

A: Local chapters of GLSTN serve several functions. We advocate for the rights of teachers who are gay and lesbian; provide a support network for them; and work to promote awareness, tolerance, and acceptance of lesbians and gays in the teaching profession. We also work to create supportive environments for students who are gay and lesbian. We present workshops, act on behalf of teachers who have experienced

discrimination or harassment, and hold meetings to provide support and plan activities.

Q: (To the school psychologist) Is sexual orientation an issue in the assessment of youngsters? Are youth who are GLB sometimes referred, inappropriately, for emotional or behavioral problems? Does sexual orientation have an impact on your diagnosis and recommendations?

A: The answer to all of your questions is yes. Sexual orientation is an issue in assessment. I know of students who were referred because of their demonstration of behaviors that are often associated with gays or lesbians. Also, students who are GLB are sometimes referred for engaging in frequent fights—because educators do not realize that these "troublemakers" actually are protecting themselves from the attacks of others. It is a case of blaming the victim. Typically I conduct an assessment over a number of days. It involves data gathering in classes, interviews with teachers, the youngster being assessed, and classmates.

Q: (To the school psychologist) If parents are unaware of their child's sexual orientation, are they informed in your meetings with them?

A: Telling the parents about the sexual orientation of their progeny has been the least of my concerns. Most parents are relieved to know what is occurring in their child's life and want to know more about how they can be supportive. I find that frequently it is the teachers who are the least supportive. When I make recommendations for better meeting the needs of students who are GLB, many teachers do not want to take ownership of their professional responsibilities. They often refuse to provide for the youngsters' physical and emotional safety as they would for other students. Many of them are not accepting of GLB youth, or they fear for their own image among colleagues and the student body if they were to support these youngsters. On the positive side, many school psychologists and school social workers conduct groups that discuss human sexuality. This provides a safe place for youngsters to ask questions, receive information, and discuss issues.

Q: (To the school psychologist) While over identification of students who are GLB for emotional and/or behavioral problems is a concern, might there also be problems with under-identification of these youth for special services? Certainly we know that the American Psychological Association no longer views a GLB orientation as "disordered," but because GLB youngsters often experience confusion and isolation and face rejection, ridicule, and attack from parents, peers, and educators, they may be in need of counseling, expanded curricula, and special programming. Should not we provide special services to some youth who are GLB, not because of their sexual orientation, but rather because of the emotional distress that re-

sults from misunderstanding and the commonly found lack of acceptance by significant others?

A: In many cases, the intervention team decides that the student in question would benefit from the ongoing psychological services provided in special education. "On paper" the services may appear to be appropriate; however, the New York City school system frequently uses special education as a "dumping ground" for "problem students," and often assigns "phantom services" (written into an Individualized Education Program [IEP], but never actually provided). Sadly, the student who is GLB may be at a greater risk of harm from other students in this environment since he or she is now enrolled in classrooms filled with unruly, and often aggressive, pupils. I hope that other school systems have more comprehensive special education programming or the ability to provide counseling without special education labeling.

Q: (To the entire panel) Have any of you had experiences with students, homosexual or heterosexual, who have lesbian or gay parents? What are their concerns, issues, and challenges?

A: When other students find out about the home situation, children of parents who are GLB often receive a great deal of verbal abuse. This ranges from ridicule of their parents and bad jokes about them, to comments that children invariably develop the sexual orientation of their parents. Again, as with GLB children who have straight parents, the emotional stress is there for both parties, but in this case the roles are somewhat reversed from what we have talked about up to this point.

Q: (From an audience member to the school psychologist) Joel, do you have much contact with youngsters who have gender identity disorder (GID)? Do you use the DSM-IV criteria to diagnose? What programming is provided for these youngsters?

A: I have had contact with a few youth with GID, and I use the DSM-IV criteria (see next question) for diagnosis. Interestingly, one of these youngsters is now taking female hormones and living as a female, still a biological male, deciding whether to undergo a transgender medical procedure. These GID youngsters often need a special setting if their behavior, mannerisms, and style of dress bring negative reactions from peers. We are fortunate in New York City to have the Harvey Milk School that welcomes these youngsters and addresses their needs.

Q: (From a student panel member) What is GID and DSM?

A: (From the moderator and the school psychologist) DSM-IV is the reference book that is used by psychologists to determine if someone has psychological difficulties in need of treatment. All the different characteristics of each condition are found in this re-

source book. Its full title is *Diagnostic and Statistical Manual of Mental Disorders, Fourth Edition*. This most recent edition was published in 1994 by the American Psychiatric Association of Washington, DC.

GID stands for gender identity disorder. It is one of the conditions described in the DSM-IV book. Simply speaking, it is when a boy truly wishes he were a girl or when a girl really wishes she were a boy. These youngsters might even go through the process of gender change when they get older.

Q: (From an audience member to the panel) With the recent research findings of elevated testosterone levels in a group of lesbians, anatomical differences in the brains of deceased gay males, and certain genes identified as having a possible influence on sexual orientation, how do we avoid falling into a medical model of identification and treatment?

A: We are educators. Our main focus should be the creation of school environments that value *all* youth. Whatever the etiology, educators must guarantee a welcoming environment for all students. Even if a particular GLB student's sexual identity is medically based, it has no medical implications for schools. Our interactions and interventions do not differ. However, perhaps there are situations in which the medical model can be of service to the GLB community in reducing prejudice from nonaccepting groups and individuals, especially those influenced by antigay biblical teachings. If a homosexual orientation could be due to a genetic or biological cause, that scientific evidence contradicts the demonic possession or "lifestyle choice" claims of the Religious Right. If God creates individuals who are GLB, then they are to be valued like God's other creatures.

Q: (To the school psychologist) What are the best ways of dealing with blame and negative reactions when a youngster self-identifies as being gay or lesbian, and when the family is nonaccepting?

A: I try to avoid the issue of assigning blame. Our role should be to empower students to make the right decisions for themselves by considering the choices available to them in their school program and by consulting their parents. However, helping parents is often more difficult. Tragically, some have cruelly rejected their child at a time when love and understanding is needed. In some cases it has been because of greater concern over what neighbors, relatives, and school personnel might say than what their youngster needs. This is where outreach and educational efforts by the school become especially important.

Q: (To the entire panel) What can educators do to support GLB students in school?

A: First, educators should treat youth who are GLB as they would any other student. (This assumes that they treat all students with respect, are concerned for their welfare, and are willing to ensure it.) Further, educators must show zero tolerance for caustic comments and aggressive actions by some students against others. Each student should be a valued individual. Human sexuality education during appropriate classes or after school can also assist students in determining their orientation and maintaining a positive self-image.

Q: (To the students) If educators and students wish to establish a Gay/Straight alliance group in their school, how would they go about doing this? What steps should they undertake?

A: As stated earlier, it is paramount that widespread support for this group be sought out and nurtured. During this time, organizers can talk with potentially interested students and faculty advisors (if they have not already been identified) about the group. Once approval has been received to start the club, organizational meetings should be held to elect leaders and decide on goals and activities. If approval is not received, awareness and sensitivity activities continue.

Q: (To the students) There are many concerned educators who would like to help youth who are GLB. If they suspect that a student might be gay or lesbian, or perhaps is developing that sexual orientation, should they approach that young adult? Should they broach the issue? If so, how?

A: It depends on the school and the people involved. If a teacher wishes to address this on his or her own, then it would be best if the educator were already friendly with the student. Otherwise, perhaps the teacher should first become familiar with the youngster and befriend him or her. Once trust has been established, the instructor might ask the young adult in a subtle way if he or she is having any problems getting along with others or is enjoying all aspects of schooling, or how that pupil is getting along with his or her parents. Directly inquiring about the youngster's emerging sexual identity is precarious.

Some schools have a designated "point person" who engages in the previously mentioned actions. In that case, teachers should notify that individual of any youngsters who might be having trouble in school or at home because of a suspected homosexual orientation.

Q: (To the entire panel) We have talked about many important issues, but now as we near the end of our time together, what is our consensus on principles that should guide us? What needs to be accomplished? How should it be done? What are the final points and recommendations that should be made today?

A: Without a doubt, the most important issue is education. If changes are going to occur to better meet the needs of students who are GLB or who are struggling with their sexual identities, we need to move students, parents, teachers, administrators, the community, and society at large further along the acceptance continuum. Education and contact with positive GLB role models helps break down the walls of nonacceptance.

RESOURCES FOR EDUCATORS

Organizations

National Gay/Lesbian/Bisexual Youth Hotline operates 7:00 to 11:45 p.m., EST. Phone: 800-347-TEEN. They also offer a pen pal service for which an application can be obtained by writing P. O. Box 20716, Indianapolis, IN 46220.

Parents and Friends and Families of Lesbians and Gays (PFLAG) offers support to family members of gay people. Its national office can refer you to local chapters. Address: 1101 14th Street N.W., Suite 1030, Washington, DC 20005; Phone: 202-638-4200.

The Gay and Lesbian Parents' Coalition offers support for gay parents and for children of gay parents, the latter through its subgroup called Children of Lesbians and Gays are Everywhere (COLLAGE). Address: Box 50360, Washington, DC 20091; Phone: 202-583-8029.

The Gay, Lesbian, and Straight Teachers Network (GLSTN) is a national organization that brings together gay and straight teachers in order to combat homophobia in their schools as well as to support gay teachers. For more information contact GLSTN. Address: 122 West 26 Street, Suite 1100, New York, NY 10001. Phone: 212-727-0135. E-Mail: GLSTN@glstn.org.; web: http://www.glstn.org/freedom/

The Hetrick-Martin Institute, a New York-based social service agency, is a leader in providing services for youth who are gay and lesbian. The Institute publishes *You Are Not Alone: The National Lesbian, Gay, and Bisexual Youth Directory*, which is available for a fee of $5.00. Address: 2 Astor Place, New York, NY 10003-6998; Phone: 212-674-2400.

The Out Youth Austin Helpline operates 5:30 to 9:30 p.m., CST. Phone: 800-96-YOUTH. Address: 2330 Guadalupe Street, Austin, TX 78705.

Books for Educators

DeCrescenzo, T. (Ed.). (1994). *Helping gay and lesbian youth: New policies, new programs, new practices.* New York: Haworth Press.

This book provides valuable information for persons who work with young people who are gay, lesbian, or bisexual and other sexual minority youth. It addresses such issues as the development of sexual identity, counseling strategies with youth who are gay or lesbian, developmental implications of homophobia for lesbian/gay adolescents, service organizations for gay or lesbian youth, and legal challenges facing lesbian/gay youth.

McConnell-Celi, S. (Ed.). (1993). *Twenty-first century challenge: Lesbians and gays in education—bridging the gap.* Red Bank, NJ: Lavender Crystal Press.

This book provides numerous ideas and resources that will assist educators in working with young people who are gay, lesbian or bisexual or who are struggling with their sexual identities. There are extensive lists of books for elementary and secondary school-aged children and youth which address such topics as famous individuals who were gay or lesbian, HIV/AIDS, developing self-esteem, and biographies. In addition, there is an extensive listing of books for educators that deal with counseling, curricula, gay or lesbian educators, and resources. There is also an extensive listing of recommended books for parents.

Selected Journal Articles on Gay, Lesbian, and Bisexual Issues*

Berrill, K. (1990). Anti-gay violence and victimization in the United States. *Journal of Interpersonal Violence, 5*(3), 274-294.

This article provides a general description of the nature and scope of violence and harassment against lesbians and gay men in the United States. It summarizes the results of local, state, and national surveys, and discusses gender and racial/ethnic differences in types and incidence of victimizations. The article examines antigay violence and harassment in such contexts as the home, schools, college and university campuses, and prisons and jails. There is a discussion of the perpetrators of antigay violence and the growing role of organized hate groups in such attacks. The article also examines time trends in antigay violence and the possible relationship between such violence and increasing public awareness about AIDS. It concludes with a discussion of the limitations of existing data and the need for greater attention to the issue.

Cain, R. (1991). Stigma management and gay identity development. *Social Work, 36*(1), 67-73.

Disclosure of homosexuality is now generally viewed in the professional literature as more desirable than secrecy: Disclosure is often seen as evidence of a healthy gay identity, whereas secrecy has come to be viewed as socially and psychologically problematic. By drawing on data from an interview study of 38 gay men in Montreal, this article shows that decisions concerning disclosure and secrecy are related to a variety of situational and relational factors largely distinct from gay identity development. It is argued that the new models of identity formation fail to recognize adequately the social factors that shape the ways gay men manage information concerning their sexual preferences. Conceptual and clinical implications of new normative views of disclosure and secrecy are discussed.

Coleman, E. (1989). The development of male prostitution activity among gay and bisexual adolescents. *Journal of Homosexuality, 17*(1-2), 131-149.

Current research literature regarding male prostitution activity is reviewed to develop a theoretical understanding of the emergence of this activity among gay and bisexual adolescents. A predisposition, resulting from faulty psychosexual and psychosocial development, appears to make these boys venerable to situational variables. More severe disruptions in psychosexual and psychosocial development seem to result in more disruptive and non-ego-enhancing prostitution activities. A clinical case study is presented that illustrates the development of such activity. Recommendations for reducing self-destructive prostitution activity among male adolescents are provided.

Coleman, E. (1982). Developmental stages of the coming-out process. *American Behavioral Scientist, 25*(5), 469-482.

Five developmental stages describing the patterns seen in individuals with predominantly same-sex sexual orientation are presented in this paper. The stages are pre-coming out, coming out, exploration, first relationships, and identity integration.

Coleman, E., & Remafedi, G. (1989). Gay, lesbian, and bisexual adolescents: A critical challenge to counselors. *Journal of Counseling and Development, 68*(1), 36-40.

Meeting the health care needs of gay, lesbian, and bisexual teenagers has become a public health imperative that challenges mental health professionals. The stigma of homosexuality often gives rise to psychosocial problems for adolescents who are in the process of sexual identity development. The stigma complicates delivery of appropriate, ethical, and sound mental health treatment. Suggestions are offered to support health development, to assist recovery from stigma, and to avert the disastrous consequences of suicide, and AIDS.

Cranston, K. (1992). HIV education for gay, lesbian, and bisexual youth: Personal power, and the community of conscience. *Journal of Homosexuality, 22*(3-4), 247-259.

Because of their behaviors and because HIV prevention programs have failed to address their unique concerns, adolescent gay and bisexual males face a higher risk of infection with HIV than most other young people. Ironically, current efforts to heighten pubic awareness about the AIDS pandemic may be nullifying the potential for gay, lesbian, and bisexual young persons at high risk to form the support networks needed to modify their behavior. The personal and group empowerment of gay, lesbian, and bisexual young people is a necessary prerequisite to their ability to make healthy behavioral choices around HIV and other health issues.

This paper proposes a comprehensive health education model for HIV prevention for gay, lesbian, and bisexual adolescents. Current health education efforts would be augmented by broader

* A special thanks to Anthony L. Menendez and Ann Fitzsimons-Lovett for helping develop this list of articles.

self and group empowerment training that would develop self-esteem, social skills, support networks, and access to risk-reduction materials. An integrated system of care involving school-based programs, multiservice youth agencies, and self-help groups would be in a position to deliver appropriate educational, mental health, medical, and social support services. Such a system of care presents gay, lesbian, and bisexual youth with their best chance to reduce their risk of infection from HIV and develop into emotionally healthy individuals.

Dempsey, C. L. (1994). Health and social issues of gay, lesbian, and bisexual adolescents. *Families in Society, 75*(3), 160-167.

Social and health issues facing gay, lesbian, and bisexual adolescents are examined in this article. These groups of teenagers often lack peer support and positive role models and thus find it difficult to establish a positive adolescent identity. Social and emotional isolation are often critical problems. Four stages of gay, lesbian, and bisexual identity development—sensitization, identity confusion, identity assumption, and identity commitment—are discussed, along with issues related to staying in versus coming out of the closet. The following health and social risks are examined: psychological dysfunction, suicide, running away, dropping out of school, prostitution, violence, AIDS and other sexually transmitted diseases. Implications for practitioners in providing comprehensive, culturally appropriate services for these individuals are presented.

Derstel, C., Feraios, A., & Herdy, G. (1989). Widening circles: An ethnographic profile of a youth group. *Journal of Homosexuality, 17*(1), 75-92.

This article introduces work-in-progress on the ethnography of a gay and lesbian youth group in Chicago. The surrounding neighborhood is sketched and aspects of the supporting agency, within which the group functions, are described. Both are seen as contributing contexts for the "coming out" process. The youth group is described in part, including age, ethnicity, and related factors of its composition. Youth are found to be involved in a process of dual socialization entailing roles and knowledge in the gay and straight normative communities.

Feldman, D. (1989). Gay youth and AIDS. *Journal of Homosexuality, 17*(1-2), 185-193.

Gay male teenagers face considerable adversity during the "coming out" process due to the AIDS epidemic. They must decide whether to be tested for HIV-1 infection, whether to postpone sexual activity, how to select a partner, and which kinds of sexual practices to engage in. Gay youth often make such decisions based upon misinformation and faulty premises. This paper reviews what is known about gay youth and AIDS and assesses their possible risk for HIV-1 infection. It is recommended that school and community-based health education programs be developed to teach gay and bisexual youth about safe sex. Moreover, research is needed into sociocultural variations among gay youth in order to develop appropriate and effective intervention strategies for AIDS risk reduction in this diverse population.

Hatcher, B. N. (1991). *Hate crimes in Los Angeles County.* Los Angeles Board of Supervisors: ERIC Document Number, ED 337 550.

A 1990 report on hate crimes in Los Angeles County (California) found 275 racially motivated hate crimes, 150 religiously motivated hate crimes, and 125 sexual orientation hate crimes. A 45% increase in crimes against sexual orientation was documented with the overwhelming number of incidents aimed at gay men. Although graffiti vandalism was the most common expression of racial and religious bigotry, assault was the most common type of sexual orientation hate crime. The report also treats crimes against women, legislation and legal actions, noncriminal acts, a discussion of why hate crimes are rising and what can be done to reduce their number, and a list of Commission actions.

Herdt, G. (1989). Introduction: Gay and lesbian youth, emergent identities, and cultural scenes at home and abroad. *The Journal of Homosexuality, 17*(1), 1-41.

This introduction opens up the field of studies of gay and lesbian adolescents, both with regard to past and present studies in the research literature, and by allusion to the new studies collected in this issue. Historical and cross-cultural elements of the context of the "coming out" process are discussed. Four preconceptions of gay youth are critically examined, namely, their heterosexuality, inversion, stigma, and heterogeneity. The anthropological construct of life crisis "rites of passage" is utilized as a heuristic framework for deconstructing attitudes regarding change and constancy in homosexual adolescents. Aspects of age, sex, class, and variables related to the form and content of the coming out process are then examined in the United States and other societies. Finally, the social problems of gay youth, AIDS, and its impact are briefly considered. The author concludes with a plea for new and urgent research.

Herek, G., & Berrill, K. (1990). Anti-gay violence and mental health: Setting an agenda for research. *Journal of Interpersonal Violence, 5*(3), 414-423.

Empirical research studies are urgently needed of the scope and prevalence of antigay violence, its mental health consequences, its prevention, and institutional responses to it. Researchers should seek data from a variety of sources, use representative samples whenever possible, use reliable and valid measures and methods, and design studies that are longitudinal and prospective. Each of these components of a research agenda for studying antigay violence and hate crimes is described.

Humm, A. (1992). Homosexuality: The new frontier in sexuality education. *FL Educator, 2,* 13-18.

This article begins with a report on school districts that are extending services to gay and lesbian youth. Recommendations on how to enhance the learning environment for gay students are presented. The article concludes with 20 common questions and answers about homosexuality.

Kourany, R. (1987). Suicide among homosexual adolescents. *Journal of Homosexuality, 13*(1), 111-117.

Little attention has been given in the professional literature to suicide among homosexual adolescents. Sixty-six adolescent psychiatrists responded to a questionnaire on the subject. Results from this survey suggest that many experts are not working with homosexual adolescents. On the other hand, the majority of those treating them considered them to be a higher risk for suicide and agreed that their suicidal gestures were more severe than those of other adolescents.

McIntyre, T. (1992). The "invisible culture" in our schools: Gay and lesbian youth. *Beyond Behavior, 3*(3), 6-12.

This article explores the various challenges faced by gay school-aged youth including verbal aggression, physical aggression, and loneliness. The role of teachers in assisting gay youth is discussed along with recommendations for improving services for gay students.

Martin, D., & Hetrick, D. (1988). The stigmatization of the gay and lesbian adolescent. *Journal of Homosexuality, 15*(1-2), 163-183.

The life of a gay, lesbian, or bisexual adolescent is one of isolation, both personally and cognitively. Gay youth often report feelings of loneliness and isolation at being different from the norm in their sexual orientation. Cognitive isolation, defined as having a lack of information on what it is like to be gay, is also another problematic area. Society, and its various components including churches, routinely reject and/or send antigay messages to these struggling youth. The implications of being gay and having violent acts perpetrated based on sexual orientation is also discussed in the article.

Nelson, J. A. (1994). Comment of special issue on adolescence. *American Psychologist, 49*(6), 523-524.

This article comments on the special issue on adolescence in the February 1993 issue of *American Psychologist.* The issues portrayed heterosexist bias because discussions of adolescent depression, substance use, homelessness, and suicide did not discuss the disproportionately high number of gay, lesbian, bisexual, and transgender youth dealing with these issues.

Price, J., & Telljohann, S. (1991). School counselors' perceptions of adolescent homosexuals. *Journal of School Health, 61*(10), 433-438.

Data from a national survey of secondary school counselors ($N = 289$) were collected regarding their perceptions of adolescent homosexuality. Most counselors underestimated the prevalence of homosexual adolescents. Almost one in five counselors reported that counseling a homosexual student concerning gay issues would not be professionally gratifying, and 20% thought they were not very competent in counseling gay adolescents. One-fourth of the school counselors reported that teachers seem to exhibit significant prejudice toward homosexual students, and 41% believed schools are not doing enough to help gay students adjust to their school environment. Perceptions of adolescent homosexuality did not vary by gender, age, or education level of the counselors.

Proctor, C. D., & Groze, V. K. (1994). Risk factors for suicide among gay, lesbian, and bisexual youths. *Social Work, 39*(5), 504-513.

Questionnaire data are used to explore risk factors for suicide among a convenience sample of 221 self-identified gay, lesbian, and bisexual youths who attended youth groups across the U.S. and Canada. Findings related to family issues, the social environment, and self-perceptions revealed a significant relationship between youths' scores and suicidal ideation and attempts. Implications for social services are discussed.

Robinson, K. E. (1994). Addressing the needs of gay and lesbian students: The school counselor's role. *School Counselor, 41*(5), 326-332.

This article explores various issues facing gay and lesbian youth, including isolation, family problems, violence, sexual abuse, and sexually transmitted diseases. The pervasive anonymity of gay and lesbian youth is attributed to homophobia and institutional discrimination. Suggestions enabling counselors to more effectively address the needs of these students are offered including practicing self-awareness, being informed of the resources available, accepting the client as a whole person, providing information, and starting support or focus groups.

Robinson, K. (1991). Gay youth support groups: An opportunity for social work intervention. *Social Work, 36*(5), 458-459.

This article explores the implications of gay adolescents who must face the primary developmental tasks of adjusting to a socially stigmatized role in American society. The difference between being gay and being a member of another minority group is discussed. People in other minority groups receive positive socialization in their early childhood experiences. The various other social challenges faced by gays are discussed including marriage, and "coming out" to family and friends. Support groups and the ways in which social workers can facilitate their development is also discussed.

Rofes, E. (1980). Opening up the classroom closet: Responding to the educational needs of gay and lesbian youth. *Harvard Educational Review, 59*(44), 444-453.

Eric Rofes, gay community activist and author, explores the issues surrounding the schools' failure to meet the educational needs of gay and lesbian youth. He argues that there has been an across-the-board denial of the existence of gay and lesbian youth and that this has taken place because "their voices have been silenced and because adults have not effectively taken up their cause." Rofes goes on the present some promising initiatives that are designed to change the status quo: Project 10 in Los Angeles and the Harvey Milk School in New York City. He concludes by proposing needed changes in U. S. schools if they are to become truly accessible to gay and lesbian youth.

Rotheram-Borus, M. J., Hunter, J., & Rosario, M. (1994). Suicidal behavior and gay-related stress among gay and bisexual male adolescents. *Journal of Adolescent Research, 9*(4), 498-508.

Adolescents are increasingly at risk for attempting suicide, particularly those subgroups who experience high stress. Typically adolescent females are at far greater risk (10.3% attempt suicide) as compared to males (6.2% attempt suicide). In this article, interview data are reported that explore attempted suicide among 138 self-identified gay and bisexual males, aged 14 to 19, presenting at a social service agency for lesbian and gay adolescents in New York City. More than 50% of attempters (*N* = 51) had tried to kill themselves more than once. Suicide attempters were more likely to have dropped out of school, to be ejected from their homes, and to have friends or relatives who had attempted suicide. Gay-related stressors were significantly more common among suicide attempters as compared to nonattempters, but general life stress was not higher. These findings imply that gay youths are at increased risk for attempting suicide.

Clinicians and staff in community-based agencies need to increase screening for risk of suicide attempts among gay and bisexual male youths and to actively seek to reduce gay-related stress.

Rotheram-Borus, M. J., Meyer-Bahlburg, F. H., Rosario, M., Koopman, C., Haignere, C. S., Exner, T. M., Matthieu, M., Henderson, R., & Gruen, R. (1992). Lifetime sexual behaviors among predominantly minority male runaways and gay/bisexual adolescents in New York City. *AIDS: Education and Prevention, 4*(3), 34-42.

Interview data are used to examine lifetime sexual behaviors among two samples of predominantly minority, male adolescents in New York City, aged 12 to 18, believed to be at high risk of HIV infection. The two samples were comprised of 59 runaway males in two residential shelters, and 60 males attending a community agency for gay/bisexual youth. Interviews regarding psychosexual milestones indicated that 93% of these youths had engaged in oral, anal, or vaginal intercourse and/or anilingus, with a median of 11 female partners among the runaway group and a median of 7 male partners among the gay/bisexual sample. Both groups initiated sexual activity at a mean age of 12.6 years. Each group reported a unique developmental sequence of psychosexual milestones. Consistent condom use was reported by 13% of the youths, while 25% reported involvement in prostitution. These findings detail the need for AIDS prevention programs targeted specifically at these youths.

Rotheram-Borus, M. J., Rosario, M., Mayer-Bahlburg, H. F., Koopman, C., Dopkins, S. C., & Davies, M. (1994). Sexual and substance abuse acts of gay and bisexual male adolescents in New York City. *Journal of Sex Research, 31*(1), 47-57.

Interview data are used to examine lifetime and current sexual and substance abuse behaviors among 131 predominantly Hispanic and Black gay and bisexual adolescent males in New York City. Results showed that many of these youths bartered sex for money or drugs. Condom use with male partners was typically initiated one year after a youth became sexually active, was more common with male than female partners, and was more common with anal than oral sex. Condoms with male partners were never or inconsistently used by 52% youths. Youths reported high rates of lifetime alcohol (76%), marijuana (42%), and cocaine/crack (25%) use. Current alcohol and drug use was significantly related to sexual risk acts. These results imply that gay/bisexual use are at serious risk of contracting HIV. HIV-prevention programs for homosexual and bisexual adolescent youth are critical and must address sex with females, inconsistent condom use, and sexual practices while under the influence of drugs and alcohol.

Rotheram-Borus, M. J., Rosario, M., Van-Rossem, R., Red, H., & Gillie, R. (1995). Prevalence, course, and predictors of multiple problem behaviors among gay and bisexual male adolescents. *Developmental Psychology, 31*(1), 75-85.

Multiple problem behaviors, stress, and personal resources were assessed over 2 years among 136 mainly Black and Hispanic gay and bisexual male adolescents (aged 14 to 19 years). Whereas sexual risk acts, substance abuse, conduct problems, and emotional distress was common, the risk acts did not form a multiple problem behavior cluster, compared with previous findings with heterosexual youths. Problem behaviors were stable over time: Only 20% to 30% of the youths changed their pattern of problem behaviors over two years. For each individual, the pattern of change in one behavior problem was not related to patterns of change in other problem behaviors over 2 years. At baseline, personal resources were associated with less alcohol use and emotional distress, and stress was associated with delinquent behaviors. The pattern of results was similar whether youths labeled themselves as gay or bisexual suggesting that problem behaviors among mainly Black and Hispanic gay and bisexual youths may follow different developmental pathways than among heterosexual youths.

Savin-Williams, R. C. (1994). Verbal and physical abuse as stressors in the lives of lesbian, gay male, and bisexual youths: Association with school problems, running away, substance abuse, prostitution, and suicide. *Journal of Consulting and Clinical Psychology, 62*(2), 261-269.

A common theme identified in empirical studies and clinical reports of lesbian, gay male, and bisexual youths is the chronic stress created by the verbal and physical abuse they receive from peers and adults. This article reviews the verbal and physical abuse that threatens the well-being and physical survival of lesbian, gay male, and bisexual youths. The response to gay male, lesbian, and bisexual adolescents by significant others in their environment is often associated with several problematic outcomes, including school-related problems, running away from home, conflict with the law, substance abuse, prostitution, and suicide. Although the causal link between these stressors and outcomes has not been scientifically established, there is suggestive evidence that these outcomes are consequences of verbal and physical harassment.

Schneider, S. G., Farberow, N. L., & Kruks, G. N. (1989). Suicidal behavior in adolescent and young adult gay men. *Suicide and Life-Threatening Behavior, 19*(4), 381-394.

This article explores the relationship of homosexuality to suicidal behavior using questionnaire responses from 52 men in gay and lesbian college organizations and 56 men in homosexual rap groups. Family background of alcoholism and physical abuse, social supports perceived as rejecting homosexuality, and no religious affiliation were associated with having a history of suicidal ideation. Suicide attempts were most often associated with intrapersonal distress.

Walters, S., & Phillips, C. (1994). Hurdles: An activity for homosexuality education. *Journal of Sex Education and Therapy, 20*(3), 198-203.

An activity designed to elucidate the various and conflicting processes of coming out is described. Hurdles are used as an analogy for the obstacles individuals face in coming out. Activity participants are given an opportunity to role-play the decision to come out and to challenge their beliefs about the simplicity of this process. Both college students and participants in professional training seminars report increased understanding and empathy for the daily "hurdles" faced by gay, lesbian, and bisexual individuals. The activity may be of particular benefit for homosexual youth.

Other Resources Of Interest

A Guide to Leading Introductory Workshops on Homophobia. Available from Campaign to End Homophobia, P. O. Box 819, Cambridge, MA 02139; Phone: 617-868-8280.

Crossroads Newsletter for people supporting sexual minority youth. Available from The Bridges Project, American Friends Service Committee, 1501 Cherry Street, Philadelphia, PA 19102.

Education report: Making schools safe for gay and lesbian youth. Available from the Governor's Commission on Gay and Lesbian Youth, State House, Room 111, Boston, MA; Phone: 617-727-3600, x-312.

Project 10 handbook: Addressing lesbian and gay issues in our schools: A resource directory for teachers, guidance counselors, parents and school-based adolescent care providers. Available from Project 10, 2050 Melrose, Los Angeles, CA 90046; Phone: 818-441-3382.

Sticks, stones, and stereotypes: Name calling prevention/intervention. Available from Equity Institute, 6400 Hollis Street, Suite 15, Emeryville, CA 94608; Phone: 510-658-4577.

Search the Internet for updated information about "gay youth." Two websites of interest are: ALLIES http://www.contrib.andrew.cmu.edu/org/allies/ Ultimate Gay Youth Page http://www.fornext.com/gayyouth/newlife.htm